NEW DIRECTIONS FOR INSTITUTIONAL RESEARCH

Patrick T. Terenzini, *The Pennsylvania State University*
EDITOR-IN-CHIEF

J. Fredericks Volkwein, *State University of New York at Albany*
EDITOR-ELECT

Evaluating and Responding to College Guidebooks and Rankings

R. Dan Walleri
Mt. Hood Community College

Marsha K. Moss
University of Texas at Austin

EDITORS

Number 88, Winter 1995

JOSSEY-BASS PUBLISHERS
San Francisco

EVALUATING AND RESPONDING TO COLLEGE GUIDEBOOKS AND RANKINGS
R. Dan Walleri, Marsha K. Moss (eds.)
New Directions for Institutional Research, no. 88
Volume XVII, Number 4
Patrick T. Terenzini, Editor-in-Chief

Microfilm copies of issues and articles are available in 16mm and 35mm, as well as microfiche in 105mm, through University Microfilms Inc., 300 North Zeeb Road, Ann Arbor, Michigan 48106-1346.

LC 85-645339   ISSN 0271-0579   ISBN 0-7879-9944-X

NEW DIRECTIONS FOR INSTITUTIONAL RESEARCH is part of The Jossey-Bass Higher and Adult Education Series and is published quarterly by Jossey-Bass Inc., Publishers, 350 Sansome Street, San Francisco, California 94104-1342 (publication number USPS 098-830). Second-class postage paid at San Francisco, California, and at additional mailing offices. POST-MASTER: Send address changes to New Directions for Institutional Research, Jossey-Bass Inc., Publishers, 350 Sansome Street, San Francisco, California 94104-1342.

SUBSCRIPTIONS for 1995 cost $48.00 for individuals and $64.00 for institutions, agencies, and libraries.

EDITORIAL CORRESPONDENCE should be sent to editor-elect J. Fredericks Volkwein, Institutional Research, Administration 241, State University of New York at Albany, Albany, NY 12222.

Photograph of the library by Michael Graves at San Juan Capistrano by Chad Slattery © 1984. All rights reserved.

TCF Manufactured in the United States of America on Lyons Falls Pathfinder Tradebook. This paper is acid-free and 100 percent totally chlorine-free.

THE ASSOCIATION FOR INSTITUTIONAL RESEARCH was created in 1966 to benefit, assist, and advance research leading to improved understanding, planning, and operation of institutions of higher education. Publication policy is set by its Publications Board.

For information about the Association for Institutional Research, write to the following address:

AIR Executive Office
314 Stone Building
Florida State University
Tallahassee, FL 32306-3038

(904) 644-4470

CONTENTS

EDITORS' NOTES

The proliferation of college guidebooks and reputational rankings has become of increasing concern to many in the higher education community. Public relations and admissions staff view such publications from a marketing perspective and the potential positive or negative consequences for enrollment. College presidents share these concerns along with the broader implications for the overall stature of their institutions. The validity and integrity of the information reported is of particular interest to those who work in the area of institutional research. Acknowledging the fact that the public, the consumers, has a great need for information about different institutions in order to make informed college choices for themselves or their children, all of these groups in higher education share alarm about the burden imposed on institutions in responding to the ever-increasing number of publishers requesting information for these guidebooks and rankings.

This volume explores some of the major facets of and issues surrounding college guidebooks and ratings. The background and development of these publications are traced, followed by discussion of major issues and perspectives—consumer use of the publications, validity of ratings, and the institutional burden of supplying the needed information. Views from both the institutions and the publishers are presented.

Despite the discussions and controversy surrounding guidebooks and ratings, there has been relatively scant research on the use, effect, and validity of these publications. Thus, one purpose of this volume is to help frame a research agenda. A second purpose is to propose a revision of current practice that will ease the reporting burden on institutions, while still meeting consumer information needs.

In Chapter One, Bruce Hunter offers a general introduction to and overview of college guidebooks. Hunter provides a unique perspective as the only author in this volume who is a practicing high school counselor. He has a long abiding interest in the subject as evidenced in his own book, *Hunter's Guide to the College Guides* (Hunter, 1994).

Reputational studies and rankings are far more controversial within the higher education community. Debra L. Stuart, in Chapter Two, describes the origin and development of these publications, highlighting some of the major issues this genre has wrought.

Given the importance, controversy, and media attention of guidebooks and rankings, it is logical to assume that there is a growing body of research describing the effect of these publications on the college choice decisions of students and parents. But as Don Hossler and Erin M. Foley report in Chapter Three, there is in fact a dearth of literature. They offer tentative conclusions about the effect of guidebooks and rankings on consumer choice based on the limited research that is available.

In chapters Four and Five, Bruce I. Mallette and Michael D. McGuire, respectively, review the two leading publications that attempt to rate and rank colleges and universities, *Money Guide: Your Best College Buys Now* and *U.S. News & World Report*'s "America's Best Colleges." These two authors explore some of the methodological concerns in each of these publications while drawing out some of the significant difficulties surrounding efforts to identify and quantify quality in higher education.

The proliferation of guidebooks and publications that rank colleges and universities has increased the demands on the same institutions to supply the raw data on which these publications are based. Anne Machung addresses this burden in Chapter Six and offers a solution in the form of a standard instrument, developed at the University of California at Berkeley, that can be submitted in response to the many surveys sent out by the publishers.

In chapters Seven and Eight publishers offer their responses to and perspectives on the issues and concerns raised in the prior six chapters. In Chapter Seven, the guidebook publishers are represented by Kimberly J. Hoeritz of Peterson's, Allan B. Corderman of Wintergreen/Orchard House, Max Reed of Barron's, and Edward B. Fiske of *The Fiske Guide to Colleges*. In Chapter Eight, the rankings studies are represented by Robert J. Morse of *U.S. News & World Report* and by Jersey Gilbert, formerly of *Money Magazine*. Taken as a whole, these responses emphasize the public's need for descriptive and evaluative information about college and universities in the difficult process of choosing which institution to attend. The publishers also express a genuine willingness to work cooperatively with interested representatives from higher education to reduce the reporting burden and enhance the usefulness of the publications for consumers.

In Chapter Nine, Josetta S. McLaughlin and Gerald W. McLaughlin attempt to digest the previous chapters and outline a future research agenda. There is still much we do not know about the effect of guidebooks and reputational studies on college choice decisions. In addition, guides and rankings for popular consumption address a broader issue as college and universities continue to struggle with the seemingly impossible task of measuring quality in the college experience.

Finally, we express our appreciation to several colleagues who have encouraged us and assisted with bringing this volume to fruition. Deb Teeter and Dawn Terkla assisted in identifying authors and reviewing early drafts. Fred Volkwein has been supportive throughout the project. We especially thank Becky Hiller for her assistance in compiling the drafts and providing word-processing support as we sought to make a whole from the parts.

R. Dan Walleri
Marsha K. Moss
Editors

R. DAN WALLERI is director of research, planning, and computer services at Mount Hood Community College, Gresham, Oregon. He is former chair of the Higher Education Data Policy Committee of the Association for Institutional Research.

MARSHA K. MOSS is assistant vice president and director of institutional studies at the University of Texas, Austin. She is former president of the Texas Association for Institutional Research and has served on the board of the Association for Institutional Research.

This overview of college guidebooks examines their origins,
development, types, impact on both consumers and colleges,
and current trends and future prospects.

College Guidebooks:
Background and Development

Bruce Hunter

The number of reference books and guidebooks targeted to college-bound students, parents, and college guidance counselors has increased dramatically in recent years. There are now more than one hundred such books in twenty different categories, and the number seems to grow larger by the day. The College Entrance Examination Board's *Annual Handbook: 1941* described that organization's forty-three member colleges and was one of the first college guidebooks. The descendant of that volume, now titled *The College Handbook,* continues to be published annually and includes some thirty-two hundred two-year and four-year colleges and universities.

Types of Guidebooks

College guidebooks can be grouped into multiple categories. Perhaps most broadly, the typology includes numbers, narrative, and strategy books.

Numbers Books. Before the early 1970s, most of the books on the market were basic references like *The College Handbook,* providing fact-and-figure data and marketed mainly to school guidance and library professionals. This category of thick, heavy books, often grouped together as comprehensive, objective guidebooks, includes *Peterson's Guide to Four-Year Colleges, Barron's Profiles of American Colleges, Lovejoy's College Guide,* and the *College Admissions Data Handbook,* and they are just as interesting to read as the large-city telephone books they resemble. Many college counselors refer to these as "numbers" books, and for many years they represented the main, if not the only, source of objective information about American colleges and universities not produced by the institutions themselves. Over the past twenty-five years, a new category of books offering narrative, subjective reviews has broadened the college reference book market, appealing to a student readership largely unreached by the numbers books.

Narrative Books. The narrative books, such as *The Underground Guide to the College of Your Choice* (Berman, 1971) and *The Insider's Guide to Colleges* (*Yale Daily News,* 1993), began to appear in 1971 and told the reader in an informal, conversational writing style "what it's really like," according to the books' authors, at hundreds of American colleges. *The Underground Guide* has not been seen since its first publication, but *The Insider's Guide to Colleges* has been joined, among others, by *The Fiske Guide to Colleges,* first published as the *New York Times'* "Selective Guide to Colleges."

The success and popularity of narrative books reflect the public's interest both in inside information and in a subjective view of how colleges have changed and adapted to serve new generations of students. Although these guides were greeted with much scorn from college administrators when they first appeared on the market, the *Insider's* and *Fiske* guides have become mainstream in recent years and are grudgingly, if not warmly, accepted by many colleges, who now view them as another college guidebook resource that students may find useful. Jon Nicholson (1983, p. 17) predicted of *The Insider's Guide* that if the next edition followed recent precedents, "the bulk of the material will be pretty accurate and it will be eminently readable." Eight years later, he called *The Insider's Guide* "well-written and informative" and "highly recommended reading," adding that *The Fiske Guide* had made many improvements since its first edition (Nicholson, 1991, p. 24).

Strategy Books. The numbers and narrative books have been updated regularly over the years and have since been joined by a number of guides written with particular readerships in mind. The ranks of these newer books include titles on college essays and applications, campus visits and interviews, college admissions strategy books, and parents' guides to college admission, and books for transfer students, learning-disabled students, student athletes, students with particular academic interests, and students with specific racial, religions, or personal backgrounds or interests.

Best of the Guidebooks

Most college guidebooks can be grouped with several other comparable books that serve much the same purpose or meet the needs of the same target market. The one volume that is considered by many to be the best book written on college admissions in twenty years is Pope's (1990) *Looking Beyond the Ivy League: Finding the College That's Right for You* (Hunter, 1994). Many college counselors quote from this work, loan it to students and parents, and recommend it more frequently than any other. It is part strategy guide, part college book for parents, and part subjective, narrative college guide. The wisdom, clarity of message, voice of experience, and sage advice to be found in *Looking Beyond the Ivy League* sets it apart from virtually every other college guidebook on the market.

The most highly regarded and widely respected college guidebooks also include *Cass & Birnbaum's Guide to American Colleges* (Cass and Cass-Liepmann, 1994), formerly known as *Comparative Guide to American Colleges,* but not to be confused with the dreadful *Lisa Birnbach's New and Improved College Book* (Birnbach, 1992). The numbers of degrees awarded by colleges and universities in specific academic disciplines in a recent year, known as the "Comparative Listing of Majors," is presented in *Cass & Birnbaum's,* making it the only comprehensive numbers book to include this feature. Many readers find the feature much more valuable than the simple lists of majors presented in many books, for, as the authors note, this listing "suggests, though it does not document, departmental strength," and "it avoids listing 'paper majors,' in which a college rarely confers a degree" (Cass and Cass-Liepmann, 1994, p. xvii).

Other outstanding college guidebook choices include the very comprehensive but costly *College Admissions Data Handbook* published by Wintergreen/Orchard House in a four-volume set, with one book for each region of the country. Wintergreen/Orchard House uses the College Research Group data base, which is widely accepted as the most complete and accurate source of such information. Several other volumes, such as *The Right College* (College Research Group, 1992) and *Lovejoy's College Guide* (Straughn and Lovejoy-Straughn, 1993), now use that data base for their own comprehensive college references. *College Admissions Data Handbook* (1994) devotes a full two pages to each college profiled, with far more descriptive and statistical detail than any comparable book. *Rugg's Recommendations on the Colleges* (Rugg, 1994), used by many college counselors to help students construct preliminary college lists, presents alphabetical lists of colleges with strong programs in specific departments, according to the author's personal research and experience. Rugg makes no effort to rank or rate colleges or departments, only to recommend colleges in several competitive groups, size ranges, and regions of the country that he feels have strong programs in certain areas. There is an important distinction to be made between books, such as Rugg's, that simply recommend colleges and those that rank or rate colleges. The fact that Rugg just recommends colleges and makes no claim of scientific or statistical accuracy has made his book a popular choice with many secondary school college counselors.

The best of the college admissions "strategy" books is *College Match: A Blueprint for Choosing the Best School for You* (Antonoff and Friedemann, 1994), published by Octameron Associates, who produce an excellent range of booklet-length publications on college admission and financial aid. *College Match* includes a number of worksheets and exercises to help students move toward the goal of finding colleges that are good matches for them, rather than providing tricks, hints, or special strategy suggestions for getting into "top" colleges. The sequence of chapters takes the reader through the college admissions process in a logical, well-ordered pattern, and the tome is both motivational and supportive throughout. A recent college guidebook for parents bears the intriguing title *College Admissions: A Crash Course for Panicked Parents* (Rubenstone and Dalby, 1994) and has been very warmly received as a patient, reassuring guide that helps parents understand the admissions process and includes a number of practical suggestions for keeping the family peace during the stressful months leading up to college admission. Table 1.1 summarizes some of the major college guidebooks by type: numbers, narrative, and strategy; rankings or recommendations; and targeting of parents.

Proliferation of Guidebooks

What brought about the kudzu-like growth in the number of college guidebooks and reference books? The public's growing awareness of the college admissions process during the late 1970s and 1980s and the "loss of innocence" that shook public faith in many institutions, including colleges and universities, were major causes. There was little demand for books dealing with the college admissions process in depth, or providing a perspective other than that offered by the colleges, before the nation's faith in higher education had been diluted by campus unrest, demonstrations on college campuses, and the Kent State shootings. The success of hundreds of new self-help books on countless topics also contributed, as writers of books for the education market quickly joined the self-help bandwagon, from glitzy titles like *Scaling the Ivy Wall: 12 Winning Steps to College Admissions* (Greene and Minton, 1987) to venerable publications like *Which College Is Best for You? A Workbook for Selecting and Getting into the College of Your Choice* (Krevolin and Smerd, 1984).

The face of American higher education changed drastically during the late 1960s and early 1970s when many prominent public and private colleges and universities became coeducational, others became integrated by legislative fiat or by institutional commitment, and colleges in general began to reflect the myriad changes in American society. The narrative books served a market niche created by students, parents, and counselors who had felt secure in their knowledge of many colleges before these institutions underwent major cultural, structural, and philosophical changes. They wanted a subjective view of how the institutions they "used to know" had weathered the storm of turbulent years.

Rankings Game

The pressures on colleges and universities to market themselves also began to accelerate during the late 1970s and early 1980s, and those pressures have continued in the face of demographic concerns, a declining birthrate, and college costs rising at nearly twice the rate of inflation. Many institutions have moved toward an enrollment management model, have embraced the business-world vocabulary of advertising and marketing, and have begun to look at college guidebooks not just as a source of general information for students but as another means of marketing their messages.

Marketing knowledge now outranks familiarity with high schools in chief admission officers' hierarchy of important characteristics for hiring admissions

Table 1.1. Typology of College Guidebooks

Type	College Guidebook (Publisher)
Numbers	*Barron's Profiles of American Colleges* *Cass & Birnbaum's Guide to American Colleges* (HarperCollins) *College Admissions Data Handbook* (Wintergreen/Orchard House) *The College Handbook* (College Entrance Examination Board) *Lovejoy's College Guide* (Prentice Hall) *Peterson's Guide to Four-Year Colleges* *The Right College* (Arco)
Narrative	*Barron's Top 50: An Inside Look at America's Best Colleges* *The Princeton Review Student Access Guide to the Best 306 Colleges* 　(Villard Books) *The Fiske Guide to Colleges* (Times Books) *The Insider's Guide to Colleges* (St. Martin's Press) *The National Review College Guide: America's Top Liberal Arts Schools* 　(Simon & Schuster)
Strategy	*College Match: A Blueprint for Choosing the Best School For You* 　(Octameron Associates) *Handbook for College Admissions: A Family Guide* (Peterson's) *Playing the Selective College Admissions Game* (Penguin) *Scaling the Ivy Wall: 12 Winning Steps to College Admission* 　(Little, Brown)
Ranking or recommendations	"America's Best Colleges" (*U.S. News & World Report*) *Rugg's Recommendations on the Colleges*
Parent target	*College Admissions: A Crash Course for Panicked Parents* (Macmillan) *The College Guide for Parents* (College Entrance Examination Board)

assistants, and the importance of educational beliefs has shown a marked drop in a three-decade longitudinal study (McDonough and Robertson, 1995). Richard Moll, author of the recently updated *Playing the Selective College Admissions Game* (Moll, 1994), *The Public Ivys* (Moll, 1985), and numerous articles on college admission, has recounted the eras of college admission from the 1960s through the 1980s as moving from "tell" to "yell" to "sell," and he suggests with "Sell, Sell, Sell" as a chapter title in his most recent book that the sell era is here to stay.

Impact of Rankings

Many colleges refer in their viewbooks, student search mailers, and promotional literature to their so-called rankings in publications like *Barron's Profiles, Peterson's Guide,* and *U.S. News & World Report*'s "America's Best Colleges" as measures of institutional quality. Too few students and parents question the sources of such information or have the courage to ignore the ratings and proceed with a search designed to find the best college match. The *Barron's* and *Peterson's*-style rankings are nothing more than the publishers' judgments of the colleges' competitiveness for admissions, usually broadly grouped as most, highly, very, less, or non, and the *U.S. News & World Report* rankings have been widely dismissed by serious education researchers since their inception (Cuseo, 1994a, 1994b, 1994c; Wright, 1990–1991). College and university admissions professionals, caught in a tight market for students, seize most any opportunity to market their institutions, and many have deigned to publish reprints of the very *U.S. News* rankings that they know full well to be flawed.

The pressures to look good in the widely read "America's Best Colleges" and other rankings publications have led some colleges to change admissions practices and to manipulate admissions figures to improve their chances of a high ranking (Stecklow, 1995). Regrettably, *U.S. News'* annual rankings have set the public agenda for determining quality in higher education, and even the most well respected colleges and universities live in constant fear that they might not rank as highly next year. Student and parent consumers who blindly and foolishly, but consistently, accept the results of annual rankings rather than conduct their own research toward what would be a student's best college match, and colleges that allow the specter of their rankings to dictate their institutional practices and procedures are helping to perpetuate what has become an annual charade in higher education.

The pressure felt by colleges and universities to market themselves to students, parents, and counselors has been matched by the pressure on students to select and gain admission to the "right" colleges that will guarantee their future success. That pressure has continued to feed the public's appetite for college reference books that produce rankings of American higher education institutions. David Webster (1984b, 1986b) has written about *The Gourman Report* (Gourman, 1993), undoubtedly the worst such ranking book on the market. Joseph Cuseo (1994a, 1994b, 1994c) has made a very strong case against college rankings, quoting research and scholarship that refutes the quality criteria used by mass-media magazines.

Real Purpose of the College Guidebooks

The most important question about the ranking books, the numbers books, the narrative books, or any of the myriad college guidebooks should be, How helpful are these books in guiding students through the college admissions process, in providing truly valuable information, and in helping students make logical, well-informed decisions that lead to good college matches? Books that suggest to students that they can shortcut the process of college research by narrowing their focus to a small handful of "highly ranked" institutions perform a disservice to students and to the many fine colleges that are not highly ranked but may nonetheless represent excellent matches for them. Books that invite comparisons of colleges on factors that have little to do with the quality of teaching and learning, or that assign arbitrary numbers to academic and quality-of-life ratings, mislead students and distract them from the tasks of critical reading and careful research that should be at the heart of a good college search. A surprisingly large handful of books on the market, including some of the most popular ranking and narrative books, are downright unhelpful, or just barely helpful, by these standards (Hunter, 1994).

The result of the proliferation of college guidebooks has been much confusion, skepticism, and mistrust among both consumers and colleges. Many students, parents, and counselors lament that there are so many books on the market they do not know where to begin, and even then, they are not sure which books are any good or will help them through the daunting process of college admission. Many college and university administrators are in a quandary as to what information they should provide to guidebook and magazine ranking publishers, and how honest they should be, unsure of how their institutions' data will be presented when the information appears in print.

Many college admission officials would prefer not to respond to information requests from publishers or publications they do not trust or respect, but as Nicholson (1991, p. 29) has noted, "Last year, 60 percent of the 4,131 presidents, deans, and admissions directors completed their [*U.S. News*] questionnaire (I'm surprised at the number who didn't—I'd be afraid not to)." The foreword to *The Princeton Review Student Access Guide to the Best 306 Colleges* tells the reader, "We couldn't get answers to *any* questions from some schools (we've excluded these schools since they have bad attitudes, and you probably wouldn't want to go there)" (Meltzer, Knower, Custard, and Katzman, 1994, p. v).

Most of the guidebooks on the market do not make clear to the reading public what they are trying to do; how they have collected, organized, and presented their data; and what the limitations of their process and publications may be. These publications should be reviewed with a critical eye. To assist, the National Association of College Admission Counselors (NACAC, 1994) has developed standards for college guidebooks that should be consulted by both counselors and students.

Computer Access to College Guides

College guidebooks have begun to appear on CD-ROMs in recent years, and perhaps that technology represents the future of the genre. *The Interactive Fiske Guide to the Colleges, Lovejoy's College Counselor,* and *Barron's Profiles of American Colleges* are now on the market at prices not much higher than their book versions. The College Entrance Examination Board, Princeton Review, and Stanley Kaplan all have programs on America OnLine and other computer online services. Peterson's has packaged an IBM-compatible disk with some of its larger books for several years now, and many major publishers have begun to consider presenting their quickly dated college and university information in nonprint formats. The number of college guidebooks has probably reached its maximum, particularly given recent technological advances and the saturation point long since reached with eight or more books in each college guidebook category. College guidebooks will continue to be a major factor in the college admissions process for many years to come, perhaps fewer in number but probably greater in variety of print and nonprint formats.

Conclusion

Guidebook publishers will gain much credibility with college administrators, students, parents, and counselors by standardizing their data-collecting and reporting formats and by ending their pointless efforts to quantify the unquantifiable by ranking colleges on grounds that change annually and fail to make meaningful distinctions between comparable institutions. Colleges and universities will recoup much credibility in the admissions marketplace by presenting their institutions honestly, fairly, and consistently, by educating the public to the flaws of rankings, whether or not their institutions rank highly, and by not accepting or reprinting their rankings as indicators of institutional quality. Students, parents, and counselors are well advised to ignore flawed college rankings and to use college guidebooks critically, selectively, and with discernment as a means toward making good college matches.

BRUCE HUNTER is director of college counseling at Wayland Academy in Beaver Dam, Wisconsin, and author of Hunter's Guide to the College Guides.

This chapter discusses the history of and issues surrounding efforts to rate and rank colleges and universities.

Reputational Rankings: Background and Development

Debra L. Stuart

Although efforts to rank American colleges, universities, and academic departments have been ongoing since before the turn of the century, their popularity and accessibility increased significantly in the 1980s and 1990s. Rankings publications differ from other guidebooks in that they judge rather than describe institutions for the reader. The public's demand for useful information and academe's concern for accuracy collide because ranking compares institutions or departments while generally ignoring differences in purpose and mission. Meanwhile, colleges, universities, and departments continue to conduct peer studies privately to compare quality. The debates on the validity of the rankings and the reliability of the data have grown louder as the public's willingness to buy these publications increases.

Definition of Academic Quality Ranking

Rankings of colleges, universities, and academic departments vary by criteria and methodology. However, to issue a ranking, as opposed to purely descriptive information, publications must assign a position to each unit on the basis of the chosen criterion or criteria. Rankings are often produced from ratings of how the departments or institutions measure on the criterion. In some cases, institutions or departments have been grouped into tiers, quartiles, or classes. For purposes of this chapter, a ranking falls anywhere on the continuum from labeling the best institutions that meet a set of criteria to assigning a specific rank to a large number of campuses or departments.

The earliest and still the most common measure of quality is reputation. Reputational studies survey experts such as presidents, academic vice presidents, deans, department chairs, admissions directors, faculty, and assembled panels. The results of the ratings collected by reputational surveys are sometimes combined with objective measures. Data are collected directly from the institutions, from other sources such as the U.S. Department of Education's Integrated Postsecondary Education Data System, or from third parties such as College Council, Market Facts, and Wintergreen/Orchard House. The rankings are based on some combination of data that have been selected to serve the purpose of the study, or they are based on the correlation with reputation.

Webster (1986a, 1992c) and Bogue and Saunders (1992) provide concise accountings of the history of rankings. This chapter includes highlights from these works.

Early History of the Academic Ranking

In 1870, the commissioner of the United States Bureau of Education began publishing an annual report of statistical data. Each year the amount of data increased and gradually moved toward a ranking by listing some institutions separately. Although this practice was dropped in 1890, the Association of American Universities (AAU) urged the bureau in 1910 to develop a classification again. Kendric Charles Babcock developed a classification scheme, but for many reasons his effort failed as a stratification and never developed into an actual ranking.

At this same time, professional associations, religious organizations, and state accreditation bodies were publishing classifications of institutions. For example, the American Medical Association's Council on Medical Education listed examination results and later added other objective criteria, including curricula, resources, and facilities. There were varying numbers of categories. In some cases these were eventually reduced to listings of approved and unapproved institutions.

Cattell's Scientists. Prior to the development of rankings in the United States, researchers in Europe were counting the numbers of eminent men who attended universities. Although cautions were written, Europeans viewed those institutions with the highest numbers as possessing the most quality. In 1910, psychologist James McKeen Cattell published the first true ranking, *American Men of Science,* based on the identification of eminent scientists and the institutions from which they had earned degrees or at which they were employed (Cattell, 1910). Cattell also calculated a ratio of eminent scientists to all faculty at each institution. Although he last published a ranking in 1933 (Cattell, 1933), his methodology remained influential until the mid 1960s (Webster, 1986a).

Hughes's Reputational Rankings. Considered the inventor of reputational rankings, Raymond M. Hughes published his first ranking, *A Study of the Graduate Schools of America,* in 1925 (Hughes, 1925). He solicited the advice of faculty from his institution for a list of raters and universities and selected twenty disciplines at thirty-six institutions (Bogue and Saunders, 1992).

In 1934, as chair of the American Council on Education (ACE) and its Committee on Graduate Instruction, Hughes improved on the first study by expanding the numbers of fields, institutions, and raters. The instructions to the raters and the listing of the institutions were changed in this second report. Instead of rating the fields on a scale of 1 to 5, the raters chose all departments that "they thought were adequately equipped for graduate work and to 'star' approximately the best 20 percent of them" (Webster, 1992c, p. 239). All adequate institutions were listed alphabetically by discipline, some with stars. Again, no institutionwide ranking was built into the design; however, as has been done frequently with such studies, others went on to produce rankings from Hughes's work (Webster, 1992c).

Manly's Newspaper Articles. "During the years 1925–1958, very few reputational rankings were published. Raymond Hughes published multidisciplinary reputational rankings in 1925 and 1934, but thereafter no major, multidisciplinary academic quality ranking was published for 25 years" (Webster, 1986a, p. 18). During this period, Chesly Manly, a reporter from the *Chicago Tribune,* brought rankings to the attention of the general public. First, he wrote a story regarding a 1946 unpublished study, conducted by AAU, designed as an internal ranking of just member institutions. Next, he constructed six rankings using consultants: "10 best universities, coeducational colleges, men's colleges, women's colleges, law schools, and engineering schools" (Webster, 1992c, p. 243).

Keniston's Contribution. "The era of the ascendancy of 'academic origins' studies and the dormancy of reputational rankings ended in 1959, when Hayward Keniston published his reputational ranking of 25 leading universities" (Webster, 1986a, p. 18). As with Hughes's first ranking, Keniston's own institution, the University of Pennsylvania, commissioned the multidisciplinary study. Unlike Hughes, Keniston surveyed only department chairs and no faculty. He combined the rankings into groupings for the humanities, social sciences, biological sciences, physical sciences, and institutions as a whole (Webster, 1992c). He then compiled the institutionwide rankings from Hughes's (1925) data.

Cartter's Report. In 1966, Allan M. Cartter, with ACE, produced the most comprehensive reputational ranking of graduate departments to date. *An Assessment of Quality in Graduate Education* (Cartter, 1966), evaluating 106 institutions, ranked departments on two separate criteria: quality of the graduate faculty and rating of doctoral training (Webster, 1992c). "The Cartter Report sold some 26,000 copies and was reviewed far more widely than any previous reputational ranking" (Webster, 1992c, p. 250).

Roose and Anderson's Follow-Up. In 1970, Kenneth D. Roose and Charles J. Anderson replicated, with minor modifications, Cartter's (1966) study for ACE. Despite its similarities to Cartter's report, *A Rating of Graduate Programs* (Roose and Anderson, 1970) attempted to minimize the importance of an absolute rank order of the 130 institutions studied.

Blau and Margulies's Professional Schools. Peter Blau and Rebecca Zames Margulies filled a void by studying professional schools (Margulies and

Blau, 1973; Blau and Margulies, 1974–1975). The low response rate on their survey of deans has been criticized. "They concluded that deans in high-prestige fields, such as medicine, responded in smaller proportions than did deans in low-prestige fields" (Webster, 1992c, p. 256). The results of their first and second rankings were similar; however, they found a relatively low correlation between the reputation of the professional school and its institution, derived from Roose and Anderson's (1970) report (Webster, 1992c).

Cartter and Solmon's Follow-Up. Allan M. Cartter teamed with Lewis C. Solmon to conduct another professional ranking in 1977 for business, education, and law. Cartter's institution commissioned the study because the board was dissatisfied with the results of the Blau and Margulies (Margulies and Blau, 1973; Blau and Margulies, 1974–1975) rankings (Webster, 1992c). The authors added faculty to the list of raters and improved the response rate. "Despite the many methodological differences between the second Blau/Margulies ranking and the Cartter/Solmon ranking, the two studies' results, for the three fields they both ranked, were reasonably similar" (Webster, 1992c, p. 260).

National Academy of Science. Although it was not designed to rank institutions, the multimeasure study of thirty-two graduate disciplines at 228 universities, *Assessment of Research-Doctorate Programs in the United States* (Jones, Lindzey, and Coggeshall, 1982), has been used to rank graduate programs and their universities. As Porter E. Coggeshall, former study director for the assessment, observed, "The primary purpose of these evaluative exercises is not to rank programs, but rather to provide useful information [and] focus attention on the importance of quality in higher education—however measured—and its multidimensionality" (1992, p. 47). The study produced standardized scores on each measure showing how far above and below each department scored on each measure. Up to sixteen measures for 2,699 programs were collected. One measure was a reputational survey of respondents from a stratified sample based on program size and academic rank. The National Research Council is in the process of replicating this study.

Recent History of Rankings

The mid 1980s and 1990s produced a period of academic quality rankings that often emphasized undergraduate education with some attention to student outcomes. At first, the audience for these rankings included academic administrators, federal agencies, state legislators, graduate student applicants, and higher education researchers (Drew and Karpf, 1981). Now the popular press has greatly expanded the audience to include anyone who reads *U.S. News & World Report, Money, Kiplinger's Personal Finance Magazine* (formerly *Changing Times*), or *USA Today.*

The public thus finds an interesting array of publications that provide some form of rankings. The criteria vary based on the authors' intent. Since 1982, *The Fiske Guide to Colleges,* produced by Edward B. Fiske, former education editor of the *New York Times,* has identified, described, and rated approximately three hundred four-year colleges and universities. *The National Review College Guide* selects fifty institutions for their general education undergraduate curricula and teaching environments. *The Insider's Guide to Colleges,* "written by students, for students," describes colleges selected for their quality. *Barron's Rating of Competitiveness* started in the 1960s, but it jumped into this newer arena in 1990 with *Barron's Best Buys in College Education.* Although the appropriate cautions are included, *Barron's* states that "the final 300 represent the best combination of sound data and student satisfaction" (Solorzano, 1992, p. v). Among the more unusual guides is "Great Ski Colleges," which lists colleges and universities near great skiing areas (Friedland, 1987).

U.S. News & World Report. Among the most controversial within the academic community and most visible to the public are the rankings by *U.S. News & World Report,* which began publishing a reputational ranking of institutions with undergraduate programs in 1983. Since 1990, the magazine has produced *America's Best Colleges,* a stand-alone publication that contains more information than is covered in the magazine. Professional school rankings were added in 1987, and "America's Best Graduate Schools" in 1992. Measures other than reputation were added to both the undergraduate and professional rankings in 1988.

Rouche and Baker's Community Colleges. In 1987, the Community College Press published one of the few rankings of community colleges. J. E. Roueche and G. A. Baker III's (1987) study identified "the top five community colleges in terms of being known nationally for success in classroom instruction" (Webster, 1992c, p. 280).

Money Magazine. *Money* has published rankings, *Money Guide: Your Best College Buys Now* (formerly titled *Money Guide: America's Best College Buys*), since 1990. Their purpose is to factor competitive cost and quality into the equation of selecting an undergraduate education. *Money's* list of one hundred institutions has attracted much attention.

Quality of Quality Rankings

The primary complaint regarding rankings of departments, colleges, and universities is that the methodology is flawed. *The Gourman Report* is generally regarded as unsubstantial and possibly fraudulent because the methodology and data cannot be verified or replicated. *U.S. News & World Report's* "America's Best Colleges" has been scrutinized, and some process and methodological changes have been made by its editor, Robert Morse. Morse has disseminated rankings data to institutions upon request, has conducted workshops to explain the methodology, and has incorporated suggested revisions from institutional researchers. *Money Magazine,* too, is criticized for using data inappropriately and having a flawed methodology. The former editor, Jersey Gilbert, responded by improving data collection and processing and by explaining his methodology in writing (Gilbert, 1992). Defenders of both publications believe that these magazines, especially *U.S. News & World Report,* are making valiant efforts to provide the public with analyses that condense hundreds of pieces of information on thousands of institutions (see Hoeritz, Corderman, Reed, and Fiske, this volume; Morse and Gilbert, this volume).

Definition of Quality. There is no consensus about how to measure academic quality; however, all of us would be surprised if Harvard and a relative handful of other institutions were missing from the top of any list. Reputation essentially has been viewed as synonymous with quality. When objective measures are used, they are compared to the opinions of experts, usually faculty and academic administrators. Although there is not always agreement between subjective and objective measures (Webster and Conrad, 1986), opinions regarding reputation have been related to size, number of "star" faculty, selectivity, citations, publications, geography, and familiarity. Bogue and Saunders (1992, p. 7) observed "a pyramid of prestige" that generally favors large research institutions. Except for graduation rates for undergraduates and job placement or fellowships for graduate students, input measures such as entering test scores and financial resources are highly correlated with reputation. A clearer definition of quality is key to minimizing bias and methodological weaknesses in academic quality rankings.

Working with available quantitative data on graduate sociology departments, David L. Tan (1992) identified factors that appear to measure quality without using reputational ratings. The author admits that "whether or not the clusters identified in the study were adequate indicators of quality remains a topic of further analysis . . . with the lack of an adequate theory of quality" (Tan, 1992, p. 218).

Rater Bias. Studies have identified rater bias among reputational survey respondents. Past affiliations influence raters' responses. The relationship between reputation and geography suggests that few faculty and academic administrators can know the quality of more than a few programs that are nearby.

Halo Effect. Sometimes departments are ranked highly because the reputation judged by faculty scholarship and perceived quality in one department spills over to other departments at the same institution. Astin and Solmon (1981, p. 17) discovered an extreme case in undergraduate programs in business that were rated highly even though the institutions had no such programs. There is also evidence that high quality is associated with large enrollments of natural science and engineering majors and low quality is associated with high enrollments of business and education majors at individual institutions. In addition, large universities that are also selective tend to be rated as the most prestigious.

Timing. Time lag between rankings presents an outdated picture of the relative quality of programs. Development of new programs and changes in established programs struggling with budget cuts that affect resources or faculty productivity are part of the current reality not represented in older studies. Also, the reverse may be true, that is, studies conducted close together influence the raters surveyed after previous rankings are reported.

Design. Attempts have been made to show changes in rankings across reports (Webster, 1983; Webster and Massey, 1992). Although interesting, the differences in methodology make direct comparisons impossible. The selection of raters and their response rates vary. Also, the wording of the survey questions differ. Some surveys include a select list of institutions, others do not. Small or innovative departments may be discriminated against because they are excluded from the lists or are relatively unknown (Webster, 1984a).

Ranking departments, colleges, and universities is like comparing the proverbial apples and oranges, especially when missions vary widely. Ranking and rating studies give minimal attention to women's colleges and historically black colleges and universities. Such studies often ignore departments with small enrollments, interdisciplinary departments, and those with interesting combinations of varying subspecialties. Applying business and management definitions of quality, Bogue and Saunders (1992, p. 11) hold the "conviction that each college and university has the potential for excellence within its own mission."

Reaction to the Rankings

The institutional impact of these ratings goes beyond the added work load described by Anne Machung (this volume). Whether it is the concern over being judged by Scholastic Aptitude Test or American College Test scores of entering first-year students or the rankings of graduate departments, higher education has responded by examining the data used to derive rankings and the way they are organized. Academic administrators are concerned about the public's use of these reports. "A little learning is a dangerous thing, both for the media and the general public. Thorough analysis over a period of time will give the most accurate picture of each college, as well as the best view of the relative merits within a group of colleges" (Wright, 1992, p. 16). "One cannot know from reputational rankings what direct educational benefit is conferred on a student, that is, whether the institution does, in fact, make a value-added difference" (Bogue and Saunders, 1992, p. 77). Although magazine editors have been accused of exploiting a market, Gilbert (1992, p. 16) argued that "Americans can easily recognize a sales pitch when they hear one. Small wonder that so many magazine and newspaper readers turn to the media with a hunger for comparative information on higher education."

Program changes occur frequently in higher education. Those initiated by reports of rankings should be consistent with the mission of the department or institution. However, Astin (1992, p. 51) found that "placing heavy emphasis on reputation-building (e.g., through aggressive hiring of stars) has generally negative consequences for undergraduate education."

Conclusion

The controversy over academic rankings is nearly as old as the studies that produced them. Before Babcock's classification of 1910 could be published, it was suppressed by two United States presidents (Webster, 1986a). The *New York*

Times made Fiske remove its name from his guide due to complaints (Webster, 1992a). The debates continue over whether these rankings should be published, who should develop them, and what is the correct methodology.

The question of whether these rankings should be produced has two distinct sides. The academic community outwardly denounces their need because accreditation determines that an institution is sufficiently qualified to educate undergraduates or graduates. However, this argument flies in the face of internal peer studies that are frequently used to establish targets or to leverage resources by departments and entire institutions. The student and parent constituencies have developed a hunger for digested information that can help them make sound economic decisions as disposable income becomes scarce and the cost of higher education increases. Assuming that rankings are going to continue, who should produce them is the next debatable point.

Historically, institutions have preferred the involvement of someone from among the fold (Webster, 1986a). Either a council (ACE) or association (AAU) has been preferable to higher education outsiders. Studies conducted at the request of an institution by one of its faculty or administrators have been suspect. Now, magazine editors are taking the lead. However, should the Student Right-to-Know Act become reality, a ranking could be produced by anyone with access to these data. The obvious concern is that individuals with little knowledge of the data will rank institutions in inappropriate ways.

"These magazine rankings succeed because so few other useful sources of information about institutions' comparative quality are available" (Webster, 1992a, p. 20). This is obviously a valid statement for a public unfamiliar with the complexities of higher education and unknowledgeable about the studies available for their reading as consumers. True student outcomes variables are more difficult and time-consuming to collect and to standardize, so they probably will never lend themselves to national rankings: "The evidence we reviewed strongly suggests that real quality in undergraduate education resides more in an institution's educational climate and in what it does programmatically than its stock of human, financial, and educational resources. That is not to say that resources are irrelevant, but that to understand educational quality one must look beyond the obvious and easy measures of institutional wealth, resource availability, and advantage" (Terenzini and Pascarella, 1994, p. 29).

Much can be measured, but the mechanism for converting data into useful information to the public needs improvement. Perhaps colleges and universities should publish their peer studies. This would satisfy the public's desire for comparisons, though the studies should relate to the departments' or institutions' missions and strategic planning. Whatever the solution, faculty and administrators must accept responsibility for institutional quality and be accountable to the public.

DEBRA L. STUART is with the Oklahoma State Regents for Higher Education.

The limited research available and the observations and experiences of admissions officers suggest that guidebooks and ratings have a small to negligible impact on most students considering colleges and universities.

Reducing the Noise in the College Choice Process: The Use of College Guidebooks and Ratings

Don Hossler, Erin M. Foley

Over the last forty years there has been a dramatic change in the relationship between institutions of higher education and their traditional clients—students and their parents. Higher education has evolved from being a privilege to a right. As competition for students has become more intense, and the marketing activities of institutions more frequent and sophisticated, the college decision has become a consumptive decision. Many traditional age students compare institutions on the basis of their locations, costs, programs, facilities, social programs, and so forth. Students are not the only ones, however, who are comparing colleges across an array of attributes. Research suggests that parents also have an impact on the college choices their children make (Hossler, Braxton, and Coopersmith, 1989; Galotti and Mark, 1994; Galotti and Kozberg, in press). Thus, while students are searching for colleges to consider and evaluating what campuses have to offer, parents are going through the same process, and, as Litten and Hall (1989) have demonstrated, the relative importance of various campus characteristics is not always the same for parents and their children.

Role of Marketing

Marketing and sophisticated recruitment techniques have become an important part of the ways in which colleges and universities identify, attract, and enroll students. Using geodemographic tools, videos, telemarketing, targeted mailings, and financial incentives in the form of both scholarships and tuition strategies, colleges and universities attempt, first, to secure consideration by prospective students and then to convert these prospects to matriculants. The higher education marketplace has become increasingly noisy; students and their families are inundated with direct mailings, telemarketers, and even television, radio, and billboard advertisements. One response of students and parents has been to seek out neutral data sources to help them sift through all of the information. They do this to help determine what individual colleges and universities really offer and to look for impartial and objective information about these institutions. College guidebooks and publications that attempt to rate colleges have thus become important sources of information for students and parents.

Studies on the relationship between college choice and marketing (Clark and Hossler, 1990; Kotler and Fox, 1985; Litten, Sullivan, and Brodigan, 1983; Litten, 1986; Litten and Hall, 1989) provide an important perspective on the college choice process. Litten (1986) was among the first to draw the attention of higher education scholars and practitioners to the connections between college choice and the service marketing literature. According to Litten, like the decision to purchase an intangible product such as choosing a doctor or joining a club, the college decision-making process has a measure of risk and uncertainty associated with it. Using the lens provided by the service marketing literature, we can see the potential value of college guidebooks and ratings.

Risks in College Choice

Choosing a college can be risky and uncertain for the following reasons. For most high school students in the United States, choosing a college is the first noncompulsory educational decision they have ever made. It is a decision for which they have had no previous practice. In addition, the parents of first-generation college students have also had no previous experience in choosing colleges. The benefits of higher education are intangible and they are not immediate; in fact, they only accrue to students over long periods of time. Furthermore, there are also great risks to students. For example, they are asked to move away from home, to leave their friends, and to enter unfamiliar surroundings. From a service marketing perspective we might view the college decision this way: "Come to Old Main, spend four years working hard. Spend $50,000 for four years, and be prepared to come to a strange and much more competitive environment. And, by the way, trust me, the benefits will accrue over a lifetime."

Consumers typically have much more experience and they know what to look for when they buy a car, when they purchase clothing, or when they eat at a local restaurant. When consumers are interested in making a more intangible purchase, they look for ways to reduce their risks, ways to make sure they are making the right choice. The more intangible, the more risky, and the more expensive the purchasing decision, the more likely potential purchasers are to seek out additional information to help them make their decisions. Viewing the college choice process from this perspective enables us to understand why college guidebooks and ratings might be an important source of information for many traditional age students and their parents.

This Chapter

In this chapter we examine the role and impact of college guidebooks and rating books on the enrollment behaviors of students and parents. Before we move on to discuss the major themes of this chapter, however, it is important to define the scope and purpose of this chapter. First, this chapter focuses primarily on the effects of guidebooks and rating books on traditional age students and their parents. Most research (for example, Hossler, Braxton, and Coopersmith, 1989; Paulsen, 1990) reports that nontraditional age students do not consider a large number of colleges and universities. Indeed, for nontraditional age students the decision to attend and the decision regarding where to attend are often the same. That is, the nearest and lowest cost college may be the only institution of higher education that nontraditional age students consider. Much the same can be said for many traditional age students who plan to live at home and commute to a nearby college or university. While these students may consider more than one college, they too tend to be very sensitive to cost and distance, thus they may not be as influenced by institutional marketing activities and are less likely to feel compelled to gather as much seemingly objective information about the institutions they are considering.

These are important caveats for college and university administrators. It might be easy for some administrators and faculty to become caught up in the "ratings hysteria" that comes around each year when rating books are published, but if the primary markets of a campus are commuting or part-time students, then the relative impact of guidebooks and rating books may be much less pronounced.

The other important limitation of this chapter is that research that focuses on the impact of guidebooks and rating books on the college decision-making process of students and parents is scant. In fact, we were able to locate only two high-quality empirical investigations that included variables that shed light on the impact of college guidebooks and ratings on the enrollment decisions of students (Galotti and Kozberg, in press; Galotti and Mark, 1994). We found no studies that focused exclusively on the role of college guidebooks on the college enrollment decisions of students. Thus, throughout this chapter, we extrapolate from more broadly based studies on the college choice processes of traditional age high school students. Clearly, given the importance many institutions are giving to guidebooks and rating books, more research is needed on the actual impact of these information sources on the enrollment decisions of students. Nevertheless, for traditional age students and their parents, there is reason to believe that they are now more anxious than in the past to find objective and knowledgeable sources of information.

Stages of the College Decision-Making Process

As we have already noted, research on the college choice process tells us little about the impact of guidebooks and ratings on the enrollment decisions of students and their parents. This statement may sound somewhat surprising to admissions professionals who are accustomed to attending numerous sessions at professional meetings in which discussions are centered on what research has to say about the impact of mass-mailing techniques, the placement of photographs and text passages in viewbooks, or how to design videotapes. While market researchers have studied these marketing strategies extensively, they do not answer the more fundamental questions about the relative importance of these efforts, or of guidebooks and ratings, on the college enrollment decisions of traditional age students.

Additionally, information can have different effects depending on the stage of the college decision-making process students are currently experiencing. For the purposes of this chapter, we limit our discussion to students who are at the point of considering to which institutions they will apply and then which institutions they will attend. Research suggests that students do not rely on written material (college catalogues, viewbooks, and other written material) extensively until they are well into the college decision-making process (Hossler, 1991; Schmit, 1991).

We do not want to suggest that information about colleges, however acquired, is not important to students. It can be very important to students. Hamrick and Hossler's (1996) study suggests that this type of information plays a critical role in helping students select institutions that provide the best student-institution fit. The authors found that college students who had reported more active information gathering during the time they were in high school were more likely to feel like they made the right choices and were more satisfied with the colleges in which they were enrolled. Thus, college information for high school students may play a key role in their subsequent satisfaction with the colleges or universities that they select. Guidebooks, however, are not the only sources of information on which students and their parents rely. Parents, and especially students, rely on a wide array of sources of information. In order to understand the impact of guidebooks and ratings we first review the range of factors that influence the college enrollment decisions of students. This provides a context for weighing the relative importance of guidebooks.

Stage at Which Guidebooks and Ratings Are Important

In order to assess the effects of college ratings and guidebooks on the enrollment decisions of students, it is first necessary to clarify when the information in guidebooks and ratings is likely to be most influential. Hossler, Braxton, and Cooper-smith (1989) noted that most high school students solidify their plans to continue their education beyond high school no later than the freshman or sophomore year in high school (predisposition stage). Although students can identify schools that they are considering attending as early as their sophomore year, Hossler, Schmit,

Vesper, and Bouse (1992), in their study of Indiana high school students, found that most students begin to seriously search and evaluate specific colleges and universities in their junior year in high school. During this time, they also begin adding and dropping institutions from the set of schools they are considering. Many students make campus visits in the late spring or summer of their junior year. Most of the students in this study made their enrollment decisions between December and early spring of their senior year.

In a more intensive study of the college choice process, Galotti and Mark (1994) looked at the intensity and focus of the decisions of high school juniors and seniors in Minnesota. They found that students were more intensely involved in the college decision-making process during the second semester of their junior year and the first semester of their senior year than they were later, in the second semester of their senior year. This seems to support earlier research that late in the junior year through early in the senior year is the most crucial time period for high school students making their final college decisions, since this is the period in which they actively seek out information about colleges (Galotti and Mark, 1994; Hamrick and Hossler, 1996).

It is important that college admissions personnel and guidebook publishers determine if guidebooks have a more pronounced effect on students when they are determining which schools they will actively consider, or if their effect is greatest among students who are deciding which schools they will apply to and attend. Answers to this question could assist institutional policymakers and guidebook publishers to determine what types of information are most useful to students and parents. Litten, Sullivan, and Brodigan (1983), for example, noted that the further students move into the college choice decision-making process, the more important factors like social environment become, whereas earlier in the process general academic reputation, distance from home, and cost are more important. Hossler and Vesper (1991) found that high school students rely more heavily on internal sources of information (parents and other family members) when they begin their college choice process (freshman and sophomore years), but then they turn increasingly to outside sources of information in their junior and senior years (peers, teachers, and counselors).

While these studies do not directly shed light on the relative impact of guidebooks and ratings, they give reason to believe that guidebooks may be most influential among high school juniors and seniors, when students and their families are in the process of dropping and adding colleges and universities to consider (search stage), and when they are determining the colleges to which they will apply (choice stage). Table 3.1 outlines the three stages of the college choice process and the most influential sources of information for each stage.

Influence of Written Material

Only recently has high-quality empirical research been conducted on the impact of written material on the college enrollment decisions of high school students. Hossler, Schmit, Vesper, and Bouse (1992) found that as early as the

Table 3.1. Influential Sources of Information for the Three Stages of the College Choice Process

Stage	Duration	Influential Sources
Predisposition	Early childhood to ninth or tenth grade	Parents and other family members
Search	Ninth or tenth grade to fall of senior year	Friends, campus visits and publications, guidebooks, and ratings
Choice	Fall senior year to spring senior year	Parents, teachers, peers, counselors, campus publications, guidebooks, and ratings

Sources: Hossler, Braxton, and Coopersmith, 1989; Hossler and Vesper, 1991.

ninth grade students start to receive information about colleges and universities. By the time these students are sophomores and juniors, they are seriously thinking about colleges and they report reading or at least scanning most of the information they receive.

The impact of this information on their actual decisions, however, is not clear. Chapman (1981), for example, found that most students used college catalogues to confirm decisions they had already made about institutions rather than to help them decide which campuses to more seriously consider and which institutions to drop from further consideration. In their review of existing research on college choice, Hossler, Braxton, and Coopersmith (1989) noted that admissions representatives and college-marketing efforts (except for financial aid offers) have only a minor effect on student enrollment decisions.

Critical Factors in Selecting a College. Litten and Hall (1989) provide the most detailed examination of the types of information students and parents find useful during the enrollment decision. They found that both prospective students and their parents think that graduate school admissions rates, academic achievements of the entering freshman class, and satisfied graduates are good indicators of an institution's quality. However, parents tend to look more at the qualifications of the faculty as a measure of quality, while prospective students focus more on the characteristics of enrolled students and academic programs offered.

Relative Weight of Guidebooks and Ratings on College Choice. Galotti and Kozberg (in press) and Galotti and Mark (1994) report the results of a longitudinal study of the college decision-making process of high school juniors and seniors. They included measures of the kind of information that students consulted and the relative frequency with which the sources were used. The most frequently consulted sources of information were, in rank order, parents, friends and classmates, students presently attending or soon to be attending colleges of interest, college brochures, and materials in high school guidance or career centers. College guidebooks were in the midrange of sources consulted but were among the more frequently used print and media sources of information. Although much more research is needed, these results suggest that guidebooks may not exert high levels of influence over students' decisions. Nevertheless, institutions of higher education are limited in the extent to which they can exert influence over parents, students, and teachers. In terms of ways to reach students and families directly, guidebooks may be one of the more effective methods. Furthermore, all of these observations cannot answer a more important question: To what extent do guidebooks and rating books exert a strong indirect effect by influencing what parents, teachers, and peers say to students when they are consulted for information? It is clear there is much we do not know about the impact of guidebooks, ratings, and many other sources of influence and information on the college enrollment decision.

Anecdotal Evidence on the Impact of Rankings and Guidebooks

Given the paucity of research on the effects of written materials and guidebooks, we also contacted admissions directors and asked for their informal assessments of the impact of guidebooks and rating books. It was a sample of convenience and no claims can be made of the representativeness of the views they expressed. However, there are common themes among their comments.

Bob Magee, director of admissions and assistant to the chancellor for enrollment services at Indiana University, Bloomington, downplayed the importance of guidebooks and ratings. He suggested that they have little effect on the college choices of students considering Indiana University. He noted that if prospective students know little about an institution, then guidebooks and ratings may be more important. He also suggested that if a school has a high degree of visibility in a region or nationally, ratings and guidebooks have little effect. Finally, he observed that only the parents of students from well-educated, upper-middle-class families buy guidebooks.

Steve Colee, director of admissions at Macalester College, claimed that guidebooks are not influential for very wealthy families. They are not important to students who attend high-status private high schools because these students receive a great deal of individual assistance from high school guidance counselors and as a result they do not need guides or rating books. He observed, however, that many good students from suburban high schools may find guidebooks and ratings useful because of the high student-to-counselor ratio.

Bob Lay, vice president for enrollment management at Boston College, said that guidebooks and ratings have differential effects. He observed that colleges may see an initial positive effect if it is the first time a college or university has received a high rating in a publication like *U.S. News & World Report*.

Continued high listings, however, have a trivial positive effect. Never being listed has a trivial negative effect, according to Lay, and a large decline in a rating has a significant negative impact on institutional enrollments.

Finally, Tom Abrahamson, former director of admissions at DePaul and current president of Lipman and Hearne, suggested that receiving high marks in a guidebook or rating book can have a very positive effect on small, less visible colleges. For larger, more visible colleges and universities, however, Abrahamson observed that ratings and guidebooks have a negligible impact on students' decisions.

Several themes are apparent in these comments. First, there seems to be a consensus that guidebooks and ratings have their greatest impact on upper-middle-class suburban high school students. These comments also suggest that smaller private and public institutions with limited regional visibility, rather than strong regional or national visibility, are more influenced by positive comments in a ratings or guidebook. Noticeably absent in any of these comments are observations about the impact of guidebooks on inner-city and rural students. In addition, there are no references to nontraditional students.

McDonough's (1994) research on the use of independent college counselors provides some possible explanations as to why some upper-middle-class families might rely more heavily on sources like guidebooks and ratings. In her research on the use of independent college counselors by high school students and their parents, McDonough (1994, p. 444) noted that "students have socially constructed themselves as college applicants needing professional assistance to stay competitive in the college access contest and have managed to create the conditions of a growth industry." We submit that these same observations help to explain why some students and parents have come to place so much emphasis on guidebooks and rating books.

We are hesitant to generalize with too much certainty about the relative impact of guidebooks and ratings on the enrollment decisions from the limited information available. It is tempting to conclude that no final statements can be offered about the impact of ratings and guidebooks on the college choices of students and parents. This option is unsatisfying, however, so we offer a series of tentative conclusions about the impact of guidebooks and ratings. These tentative conclusions can best be viewed as a series of hypotheses to be tested rather than as a set of definitive judgments.

The limited research available and the observations and experiences of admissions officers suggest that guidebooks and ratings have a small to negligible impact on most students considering colleges and universities. The inferences from other studies suggest that nontraditional and commuting students are not influenced by guide and ratings books. In addition, it appears that low-income and first-generation college students are less likely to be influenced by or rely on guidebooks. If Steve Colee of Macalester College is correct, high-income students may also not rely greatly on guidebooks and ratings. This suggests that only middle-income students are extensively influenced by guidebooks and ratings. In addition, it may be that those middle-income students considering smaller private and public regional institutions are most likely to use ratings and guidebooks.

Final Thoughts

In total, there remain many unanswered questions about the impact of guidebooks and ratings on the college choices of students. Research to date suggests the impact of these sources may be small. There is some reason to question why guidebooks and ratings have received so much attention in recent years in light of their limited impact on the decisions of students and parents. Nevertheless, given the ambiguities and uncertainties for both students and parents, as well as institutions, it is perhaps not surprising that ratings and guidebooks have received so much attention.

From an institutional perspective, even though researchers have greatly expanded our understanding of the college choice process and how colleges and universities can intervene to influence this process, the fact remains that researchers can still not accurately predict in advance the precise colleges in which students will choose to enroll. Many admissions officers are still not sure which of their marketing and recruitment activities really work and which of them have only a marginal effect, or no effect. In the midst of these doubts, guidebooks and ratings can serve as one more source of uncertainty reduction, something more tangible for admissions officers to point to in explaining their success or failure in attracting the right number of students with a desirable set of academic and nonacademic attributes.

From the perspective of students and parents, sizable numbers of them purchase guidebooks and rating sources each year. For many students and their families, these guidebooks may have little impact or serve only as confirmatory devices, helping them to feel comfortable with decisions they have already made. However, for middle- and upper-middle-class students and parents, especially those considering regional private and public institutions, ratings and rankings may be important sources of information that help to eliminate some colleges and universities from further consideration, while elevating others for further evaluation.

Despite the apparently restricted influence of guidebooks and ratings on most students and parents, it is likely that they will continue to be published. To paraphrase McDonough's (1994) observations about independent college counselors, these publications have become a growth industry.

As long as guidebooks are published and used, it is incumbent upon both institutional administrators and publishers to provide timely, accurate, and useful information. Hossler and Litten's (1993) detailed study of guidebooks and college-rating schemes offers insights that merit consideration. They discuss the results of a study conducted by Pollock (1992) in which he found many inaccuracies and conflicting information in the guidebooks he reviewed. He suggested that some of the information may be the result of intentional efforts by some campus administrators to not provide totally accurate information, or the inaccuracies may simply be due to a failure to carefully monitor and cross-check information provided.

Hossler and Litten (1993) also noted that many guidebooks and rating books make evaluative statements about campuses without providing any information as to how they secured their data. These researchers urge readers to be cautious about attaching too much importance to any guidebook that does not explain in detail how the compilers collected information about the colleges and universities discussed. Finally, they concluded that most guidebooks are not organized or written in a manner that meets the needs of students. For the most part, guidebooks are constructed around information that institutions provide, rather than around information independently gathered and organized in a manner that is most useful to students and parents.

Hossler and Litten (1993) give generally high marks to *U.S. News & World Report*'s "America's Best Colleges" and to *Money Guide: Your Best College Buys Now*. However, even with these publications, they point out several problems. Nevertheless, college guidebooks and ratings are here to stay. It is important for college and university administrators to understand what kinds of students are most likely to rely on them and whether their individual campuses are likely to be influenced by guidebooks and college ratings. Future research on the effects of guidebooks and ratings should examine both their direct and indirect effects on students, parents, educators, and peers.

DON HOSSLER is professor and chair in the Department of Educational Leadership and Policy Studies at Indiana University, Bloomington.

ERIN M. FOLEY is a doctoral candidate in the Department of Educational Leadership and Policy Studies at Indiana University, Bloomington.

An examination of popular publications that rate and rank collegiate undergraduate education reveals several methodological concerns. The challenges for consumers and researchers are to know what shortcomings exist in these ratings, what impact these shortcomings have on the rankings, and what methodological changes might improve the evaluations.

Money Magazine, U.S. News & World Report, and Steve Martin: What Do They Have in Common?

Bruce I. Mallette

"The new phone book's here! The new phone book's here!" This famous movie line is exclaimed by Navin R. Johnson, played by Steve Martin in *The Jerk*. As Navin excitedly dances about the gas station where he works, he expresses how he is now someone because he is listed in the new phone book. Navin shouts, "I'm SOMEBODY now! Millions of people look at this book every day! . . . I'm in print. Things are going to start happening to me now."

This scene is often reenacted when the college rankings on undergraduate education are released by *Money Magazine* (*Money Guide: Your Best College Buys Now*) and *U.S. News & World Report* ("America's Best Colleges"). Navin R. Johnson's reincarnation in campus administration buildings is confirmed when the hallways of academe echo with the words, "The rankings are out, the rankings are out." Navin's phone book listing amid thousands of names is to his sense of identity and worth what an appearance in the college rankings is for hundreds of institutions.

College Rankings, Media, and Campus Reactions

Today's smorgasbord of collegiate rankings and ratings feed the appetite of America's newsstands, and college officials eagerly wait to review the new menus. Chief executive officers, provosts, and admissions directors are known to feverishly flip through the publications' pages seeking their latest stature among the hundreds of institutions of higher education. College and university officials often find themselves in a dilemma. On the one hand, rankings "may indicate [an institution's] trajectory and popularity but are rarely meaningful" and, on the other hand, "prospective students carry lists around with them as guides to where to apply" (Theus, 1993, p. 285). Because of this dilemma, the campus version of Steve Martin's Navin-like ritual started across American campuses with the publication of *U.S. News'* first set of rankings in "America's Best Colleges" in 1983, and it intensified when *Money* jumped into the competition in 1990 with its *Money Guide: America's Best College Buys* ratings.

The release of the fall rankings are just the first stage of media attention and public discussion of quality, cost, and value in undergraduate education. After the various rankings are released, wire services quickly pick up the story and news items appear across the nation. Local television stations start creating sound bites for the evening news and editorial page columnists shift into a higher education commentary mode. One columnist correctly acknowledged, "One year's worth of magazine ratings might not prove a whole lot no matter how carefully they are compiled," but he concluded, "Trends can be more revealing . . . [because] you can see who's hot and who's not" (Ford, 1994).

The coverage of the rankings does not end immediately after the initial early fall commentaries are over. CBS got into the action during its December 1994 coverage of the Division I-AA football championship when it observed that the university hosting the game was one of the top five best buys in the South. Alumni magazines generate stories to either applaud their rankings or to explain them. Wake Forest University explained the impact of the institution's reclassification from a regional to a national university in the first issue of its alumni magazine after the *U.S. News* rankings were released ("First Tier . . . ," 1994). *Money* revisited its fall 1994 value rankings in its January 1995 issue by using four of its quality variables to determine how the top twenty-five football schools perform academically (Kasky, 1995).

Fulfilling Expectations of Accuracy

The public entrusts to *Money* and *U.S. News* an expectation of accuracy. This expectation applies to an informed and meaningful interpretation of how to assess the quality and costs of undergraduate education, and to the ability to collect and analyze appropriately the data used in the numerous pages of evaluation tables published in their guides.

Publishers must meet four basic challenges to fulfill these two expectations of accuracy: (1) The constructs of quality and cost must adequately represent their complexities, (2) the institutional data collected must adequately represent and measure the chosen constructs of quality and cost, (3) the measures must be representative of the broad and diverse spectrum of higher education institutions, and (4) the measures must not be burdensome for institutions to provide.

Which Institutions Are Rated and Ranked?

American higher education's diversity is represented by 1,402 four-year institutions, 512 public and 890 private (Carnegie Foundation for the Advancement
of Teaching, 1994). This total excludes specialized institutions (that is, institutions awarding at least 50 percent of their degrees in a single discipline) and
tribal colleges and universities. Just as the "March Madness" of the National Collegiate Athletic Association (NCAA) begins with a field of sixty-four men's basketball teams, *Money* and *U.S. News* select a pool of schools and the competition
begins. Each selects for their analyses a slightly different institutional population from this universe of schools.

Money includes 959 schools in their "value" ratings to generate the top
100 "best buys." They also share vital data on, but do not rank, 1,010 four-
year schools, of which the 959 schools evaluated for value are a subset (*Money
Guide . . . ,* 1994). *Money's* exclusion of approximately 400 schools from the
four-year school universe is based on multiple criteria: (1) Only the "leading"
institutions are examined; (2) 150 schools do not qualify for the analysis that
determines the 100 best buys since they are service academies or highly specialized colleges, they require students to work, or they have at least 45 percent part-time enrollments; and (3) the institutions are religious schools, as
determined by *Money* after examining the mission statements and the speci-
ficity of required religion courses.

U.S. News rates and ranks 1,416 institutions of higher education ("America's Best Colleges . . . ," 1994). Its rankings include 90 specialty schools (43
in arts, music, and design; 33 in business; and 14 in engineering) but exclude
schools with enrollments of fewer than two hundred students. Thus, *U.S. News'*
institutional population is approximately the complete universe of four-year
schools. The institutional classification categories of the Carnegie Foundation
for the Advancement of Teaching are used by *U.S. News* as the basis for placing the rated schools into school groupings. The nine core categories of the
Carnegie classifications are condensed to form a typology consisting of five
school groupings (national universities, national liberal arts colleges, regional
colleges and universities, regional liberal arts colleges, and specialty schools).

The methodologies and specific variables used by *Money* and *U.S. News*
in conducting their ratings and rankings are subject to criticism since they
sometimes fall short in meeting the two expectations of accuracy discussed
earlier. The following sections of this chapter focus on basic concerns with
Money's approach to ratings and other unresolved issues for all publishers in
the rating-and-ranking business.

Money's "Best Buys": How Much Quality for the Cost?

Money's niche in the college ratings market is to identify "the schools that
deliver the highest-quality education for the tuitions they charge" (*Money*

Guide . . . , 1994, p. 21). *Money* acknowledges that its "statistical analysis necessarily requires setting some working definitions that deal with gray areas" (Gilbert, 1992, p. 35). However, *Money*'s published "working definitions" are incomplete and the "statistical analysis" techniques remain unknown to the readership.

From its inception, mystery surrounded the *Money* guide's approach. "Perhaps the most serious problem is the methodology is not explained, i.e., there is no way for the reader to really understand the data and draw independent conclusions from them" (Wright, 1992, p. 12). This concern remains valid since the most current issue of *Money*'s guide also does not disclose the complete variable definitions and statistical methods used to generate the rankings. The broad descriptions of the sixteen quality variables and five cost variables provide limited information and raise concerns of construct validity. Table 4.1 lists the quality variables and the "vital data" variables used by *Money*. The following discussion focuses on four of *Money*'s quality variables and three of the vital cost variables.

Faculty Deployment.   This variable is defined as "the ratio of students to tenured faculty who actually taught classes in the fall of 1993" (*Money Guide . . . , 1994, p. 21). *Money* believes the lower the ratio the better. This assumes educational quality is a function of exposure to tenured teaching faculty. This may or may not be true. Schools without traditional tenure, such as Hampshire College and Evergreen State College, cannot be said to be absent of quality. As schools reduce tenure track positions and create alternative tenure track policies, the nature of faculty will continue to evolve (Chait, 1995).

As currently defined, faculty deployment represents simply the ratio of students to tenured teaching faculty. It does not represent the deployment of tenured faculty to teaching since the definition is based on "classes" and not "undergraduate course instruction." In addition, there is no ratio provided of tenured faculty teaching to tenured faculty not teaching. If this variable is kept in future analyses, then its name should be changed to more accurately reflect what it does represent.

Instructional Budget.   *Money* created this expenditure-per-student variable by using information from United States Department of Education reports. *Money* does not explain which reports and data were used to create the per student amount or the year of the data. (If the reports are from the Integrated Postsecondary Education Data System, then they are based on old data.) If we assume that reports on institutions' instructional expenditures were used, then the data are problematic.

Graduate and professional school costs per student are usually higher than undergraduate costs per student. Therefore, institutions with large graduate or professional school programs that are located in areas with a high cost of living receive a benefit in institutional comparisons of instructional budgets. In fact, California Institute of Technology, where over 50 percent of students are graduate students, rated first on this variable. An adjustment to account for the size of a school's graduate and professional programs is needed. In addition,

Table 4.1. *Money's* **Measures of Educational Quality and Vital Data**

Educational Quality	Vital Data in Guide Section
Entrance examination results	Tuition and fees
Class rank	Room and board
High school grade point average	Percentage of undergraduates receiving
Faculty resources	financial aid
Core faculty	Percentage of need met
Faculty deployment	Average gift aid per student
Library resources	Student/faculty ratio
Instructional budget	Percentage who graduate in six years
Student services budget	Student academic level
Freshman retention rate	
Four-year graduation rates	
Five- and six-year graduation rates	
Advanced study	
Default ratio on student loans	
Graduates who earn doctorates	
Business success	

Source: Based on *Money Guide . . .* , 1994, pp. 21, 71.

undergraduate program costs differ. For example, engineering and sciences are much more expensive to support than humanities.

Business Success. Standard and Poor's listing of where 71,500 top executives went to college was used to define "business success." The majority of top executives have been out of college for a number of years and their numbers of women and minorities are underrepresented. Therefore, this variable has an inherent problem of an incomplete representation of the success construct.

This point was supported by results of the Glass Ceiling Commission, a twenty-one-member commission appointed by Congress and the Bush administration and made up of lawmakers, corporate executives, and representatives of public interest groups. After three years of study, the commission concluded that efforts to break the glass ceiling that keeps women and minorities from the upper echelons of the corporate world are "disappointingly slow" (Swoboda, 1995). The commission reported that even though 57 percent of the work force is female or minority, only 5 percent of the top managers of Fortune 2,000 industrial and service companies are women, and most of them are white. Within the Fortune 1,000 industrial corporations, 97 percent of senior managers are white males. The problem is greater than just numbers, it is attitude. The report stated, "The overwhelming number of CEOs interviewed . . . think of the glass ceiling as something that used to affect women—white and non-white—but that is no longer a real problem for them" (Swoboda, 1995, p. A1). In an effort to acknowledge women and minorities, *Money's* 1994 issue lists the top ten women's colleges (representing 11.9 percent of all women's colleges) and the top five historically black colleges and universities (HBCUs) (representing 5.6 percent of all HBCUs). However, this attention is lost in the composite rankings since the business success focus on the corporate sector inadequately represents the civic and social contributions of these institutions' graduates.

Fortunately, other print media have recently had comprehensive articles on women's colleges (Gose, 1995; Reeves and Marriott, 1994; Talbot, 1994) and the publication *Black Issues in Higher Education* regularly addresses issues related to HBCUs. If *Money* continues using business success as currently defined, then the reader should be informed of the limitations and bias of the variable.

Library Resources. The definition of library resources is the total of a school's reference materials (books, periodicals, and microfilm) divided by the number of students using the campus libraries. This variable becomes increasingly weaker as technology advances. For example, a student at North Carolina State University, North Carolina Central University, Duke University, or the University of North Carolina at Chapel Hill can access any of the four card catalogues electronically. In addition, these students can gain access to the libraries of five other area colleges and universities. Similar technology and exchanges exist at hundreds of other colleges nationally. The access of college students to library resources is much more extensive than represented by the current definition of the variable. This variable would be improved if those library resources that can be accessed within a reasonable period of time were included. Schools making improvements in their library science technology to enhance student access to information would benefit with this definitional change and those schools not moving with technology would fall farther behind.

Percentage of Undergraduates Receiving Financial Aid. The presentation of the vital data tables on 1,010 schools implies the higher the percentage of undergraduates receiving financial aid the better. This percentage does not distinguish among the sources of aid received, that is, grants, scholarships, work, and loans. In general, a lower-cost school will have a lower percentage of students receiving aid since their estimated financial need will be less if the school costs less.

The most preferred type of aid is gift aid (grants and scholarships) since these awards are not repaid. Campus work programs, either institutionally based or the federal work-study program, are another means to receive aid. Two important questions about work programs are, What is the average work award? and What is the average number of hours of work per week required? Without these two pieces of data, it is difficult to know if the aid earned is worth the amount of time needed to earn it. Even campus averages mask the range in hourly pay rates that may exist on a campus.

Another category of aid is loans. Loans can be need-based or non-need-based. In general, need-based loans accrue no interest if the student is enrolled, whereas non-need-based loans accrue interest while the student is enrolled. Thus, need-based loans are less expensive than non-need-based loans. *Money's* current definition of this variable would be greatly improved if it was sorted into the various sources of financial aid.

Percentage of Need Met. This percentage more closely measures the relationship of need, aid, and cost since it serves as a broad proxy for how much need remains to be covered. The problem with this variable is the same as that of the previous variable, that is, need can be met through several basic means and some means are financially more attractive than others.

Tuition and Fees. For the public institutions reviewed, out-of-state tuition and fees constituted the measure for cost. This presents two problems. First, this definition does not match the financial aid data analyzed— percentage of undergraduates receiving financial aid and percentage of need met. These two financial aid variables represent all undergraduates, both in-state and out-of-state. Therefore, the definition of cost (which uses out-of-state data) is combined with financial aid need (which uses in-state and out-of-state data). This definition mixes apples and oranges in the analysis. For out-of-state cost to be the appropriate cost measure then, out-of-state financial aid data must be used as the appropriate aid measure for determining the average amount of financial need met.

A second concern with the current definition of cost is its disregard for students remaining in-state and attending public colleges and universities. This concern is extremely important since the national average for all first-year students in four-year colleges who graduated from high school in the prior twelve months and enrolled in-state is 74 percent (National Center for Education Statistics, 1994, p. 206). Twenty-four states have percentages higher than the average. *Money* does provide a short list of twenty-two "top public schools ranked by in-state tuition" (*Money Guide . . .*, 1994, p. 17), but this focus is lost in the central table of 1,010 schools. An in-state reader may make a "value" conclusion based on a school's listing in the central table unless the small table of the top twenty-two public schools is found in the guide. Many states are rapidly increasing out-of-state tuition, and there may be a growing trend to attend an in-state public school. *Money* needs to provide data to reflect this consumer need.

Money could resolve this problem with a change to a dual ranking for public schools in the guide's central table. For example, public college X might receive a ranking of 23/98, where the first rank indicates its in-state value based on in-state tuition and fees, and the second rank represents its out-of-state value based on out-of-state tuition and fees. In the absence of adequate information regarding in-state value, many public schools will be rated and ranked on cost and financial aid factors that impact only a small minority of their new first-year students and total undergraduate enrollments.

Money's Claims: Public Beware

A major concern with *Money*'s guide involves the claims made regarding the ratings and rankings. The claims made in the guide's headlines are difficult to accept even if *Money*'s definitions and methodologies are assumed to be correct. The cover of the 1994 issue declares, "All the Key Facts You Need on 1,010 Four-Year Schools," not helpful, useful, or important facts but "all" key facts. Such absolute claims seem more understandable in a supermarket tabloid than in *Money*. In reality, only three of the "vital data" variables in the table of

1,010 schools (percentage of undergraduates receiving aid, percentage of need met, and average gift aid per student) require any analysis to be created. The other five variables presented are basic information found in institutional admissions literature and other college guidebooks.

Another *Money* claim is "Whatever your needs, you're likely to find a school that fits them among our top 10" (*Money Guide . . .* , 1994, p. 23). Ten schools do not cover the gamut of students' needs. The missions, curriculum offerings, campus environments, costs, locations, and sizes are far too diverse to offer such a simplistic conclusion. *Money* also claims to have discovered through "value analysis" that out of 78 schools charging more than $17,500 in tuition and fees, "only 16 are worth it" (*Money Guide . . .* , 1994, p. 16). No definition of "worth" is provided nor is an explanation of what "worth" cutoff point was used to separate the 16 chosen schools selected from the other 62 schools in this category.

Money also selects 26 schools representing the state schools with the best honors programs. Again, no definition of "best programs" is provided. No public HBCUs are listed among the 26 schools. The absence of any focused information on four-year HBCUs, public ($N = 40$) or private ($N = 49$), is a major shortcoming to *Money*'s claims of providing "all the key facts you need" in deciding on a college. Recent national data indicate four-year HBCUs enrolled 28 percent of all African Americans enrolled in four-year schools and awarded 27.6 percent of their bachelor's degrees. This was the third consecutive annual increase in degrees conferred to African Americans by HBCUs and the highest percentage since 1988–1989 (Carter and Wilson, 1995, p. 18). An important source of information on minority degree generation is "Top 100 Degree Producers," published annually since 1992 in *Black Issues in Higher Education* (for example, "Top 100 Degree Producers," 1995). This source provides rankings that minorities cannot find in *Money* or *U.S. News*.

Even though HBCUs are an important part of higher education's diverse offerings, there is limited information in *Money*'s guide. For example, comparisons of the academic performance, economic benefits, educational attainment, and identity development of African Americans at HBCUs versus majority institutions are not addressed. As Terenzini (1994, p. 4) concluded, it is a myth that HBCUs "do not provide as effective an education for black students as do predominantly white institutions." *Money* could complement the scope of its rankings by reviewing Fleming (1984), who discusses the impacts of HBCUs and white institutions on African Americans, and Pascarella and Terenzini (1991), who provide a brief overview of the major research in these areas.

Ratings and Rankings: Continuing Issues

The prior discussion of concerns about the methods and design of *Money*'s "best college buys" presents recommendations for specific changes. In addition, there are other concerns that *Money*, *U.S. News*, and other rating-and-ranking publishers must resolve.

Data Integrity: How Can Cheating Be Eliminated? Stecklow (1995), in a feature article in the *Wall Street Journal*, warned that all is not well in the data submitted by schools to *U.S. News* and *Money*. Through a series of comparisons using data from *U.S. News, Money,* Moody's Investors Service, the NCAA, and Standard and Poor's, he demonstrated that numerous schools inflated Scholastic Aptitude Test (SAT) scores and graduation rates while lowering acceptance rates. Most surprising were quotes from several campus administrators who admitted to the deliberate alteration of data submitted to *U.S. News* in an effort to enhance their campuses' rankings. The article hit a nerve. The *Wall Street Journal's* "Letters to the Editor" in response to the article brought comment from *U.S. News'* managing editor explaining how the magazine planned to tighten data integrity controls. In addition, two college presidents and one dean defended their institutions from the accusations of cheating, and two other senior college staff voiced disdain for colleges who do cheat ("Letters to the Editor," 1995).

The debate surrounding the degree of integrity in institutional data provided to the public is not new. An article in the *New York Times* on "hyping numbers at colleges" had appeared only three months prior to the *Wall Street Journal* piece (Knowlton, 1995). In fact, back in 1987, the *New York Times* raised the question of schools inflating SAT scores for marketing reasons (Carmody, 1987). The problem was well summarized by one university president, who said, "The adoption of Madison Avenue techniques to promote our institutions, and the consequent decline in—or loss of—our collective integrity" (Gilley, 1992, p. 11) was one of the excesses of the 1980s. Stecklow (1995, p. A1) concluded that these excesses continue: "In their heated efforts to woo students, many colleges manipulate what they report to magazine surveys and guidebooks—not only on test scores but on applications, acceptances, enrollment and graduation rates."

The responsibility for honor and integrity in data accuracy clearly rests with campuses. However, *U.S. News* and *Money* do have important roles to play. Data edits are needed to identify when a school's data on a specific variable changes more than would be statistically likely from one year to the next. It is imperative for guide publishers to work with institutional research professionals to define appropriate parameters for identifying unacceptable variances in data submissions.

Full Disclosure of Rating and Ranking Methodologies. A standard for article publication in academia is a thorough disclosure of methodology to assist the reader in evaluating the merit of the published results. The full methodologies used to establish rankings by *U.S. News* or *Money* are not published. The magazines contend page space is a constraint and only a limited amount of methodological information can be printed. *U.S. News* continues to release increasingly more of its methodology to the public each year, while *Money* publicly discloses very little about its methodological magic.

The views of the two magazines regarding their current levels of methodological disclosure are far from realistic. *Money* stated in its 1994 issue, "Here's how we chose the 10 best buys in higher education . . ." (*Money Guide . . . ,* 1994, p. 21) and then provided partial variable definitions and absolutely no methodological explanation. *U.S. News'* managing editor, responding in a letter to the editor in the *New York Times* about an earlier article that referenced the *U.S. News* guide, wrote, "If you had read our methodology, which we detail in our guide, you would have found out what our weights are. The acceptance rate counts for a small fraction of a school's overall ranking" (Sanoff, 1995). In reality, the *U.S. News* guide only printed the weights of the six core factors and not the core factors' seventeen subfactors, of which "acceptance rate" was one. Thus, the managing editor's public letter is inaccurate.

Magazines are in the business of making revenue. However, the addition of one or two pages of detailed methodological description in the annual guide will not break their banks. Is the issue truly page space availability or is it a decision by each magazine's leadership to not explain to readers how the rankings were determined and thereby also keep their methodology from their publishing competitors? True, all readers do not need a detailed statistical description of the ratings. For those readers who do seek these details, the magazines should provide addresses where a full statistical description of the methodologies can be obtained. However, the average reader does need more explanation than what is currently disclosed. In its absence readers will make sweeping conclusions based on little information.

Publishers should also provide historical charts of the subfactors (and weights) used to establish the rankings. This type of chart would help explain how the guide has changed over time. There is also a problem of interyear ranking comparisons. The magazines should make no reference to a school's movement up or down in the rankings from year to year since noncomparable methodologies make such statements meaningless and mislead the reader. Only a limited amount of year-to-year comparisons are currently published, but these still suggest that a change in the rankings is based on a change in quality or value.

Where Do We Go from Here?

Publishers want to produce newsworthy articles, issues, and guides to increase their revenues. *U.S. News'* "America's Best Colleges" and *Money's Money Guide: Your Best College Buys Now* are for them what the "Swimsuit Issue" is to *Sports Illustrated*—high gloss, high profile, and everyone wants to look at it. Similar to *Sports Illustrated, U.S. News* and *Money* represent only a specific aspect of the full story. Whereas *Sports Illustrated* seeks only the most popular models to adorn swimwear, *U.S. News* promotes a methodology highlighting schools with the most established reputations and wealth, and *Money* claims to have found the answer to how good an education one gets for each dollar spent. The annual college rankings of undergraduate education create a "Fall Fever" not too different from the "March Madness" surrounding the NCAA basketball tournament, and it spreads rapidly.

U.S. News and *Money* will continue to produce their ratings and rankings since it would be economically foolish for them not to do so. However, responsible journalists, like responsible educators, have an obligation to continue to seek a better understanding of the product they evaluate and to better inform the public as to their findings. The research directors of each magazine have become more receptive to asking for input from the higher education community and seeking a dialogue on methodological issues and concerns. However, it is the magazines' senior editors who need to become cognizant of the broader research issues and permit their research directors to truly seek improvements in rating and ranking methods.

Challenges. The search for methodological improvements will continue, but the creation of a widely accepted format will be a formidable challenge. As Rich (1995) has commented, "Distinguishing between one institution and another (quantitatively) . . . is a futile exercise which does not adequately account for qualitative and 'cultural' factors, yet despite US News' warnings, the public (and even institutional administrators) believe there are meaningful differences between one rank and the next."

Other criticisms of the ratings have less to do with methodologies than with "the variables they use in the first place—none of which is closely related to learning gains once students' precollege characteristics are controlled" (Pat Terenzini, personal communication, April 14, 1995). "Nearly all the variance in learning and cognitive outcomes is attributable to individual aptitude differences among students attending different colleges. Only a small and perhaps trivial part is uniquely due to the quality of the college attended" (Pascarella and Terenzini, 1991, p. 592).

Helpful Resources. In an effort to overcome these challenges and better understand the product they wish to evaluate, journalists should return to the skills they expect of their readership—read and reflect. Three books should be required reading of any staff member working on ratings and rankings: Boyer's (1987) *College: The Undergraduate Experience in America,* Pascarella and Terenzini's (1991) *How College Affects Students: Findings and Insights from Twenty Years of Research,* and Astin's (1992) *What Matters in College: Four Critical Years Revisited.*

Boyer's (1987, pp. 286–297) eighty-six questions on undergraduate education can serve as a good starting point for magazine publishers to review and revise their conceptual frameworks. While answers to all of Boyer's questions are not easily collected in the form of data, they do represent a holistic framework for the consumer to explore campus quality. Pascarella and Terenzini's (1991) review of research on how colleges make a difference provides a rich discussion and summary of myriad topics. Astin's (1992) empirically driven research is a fertile source on many important educational issues.

A New Player in the Quality Arena. The debate surrounding the characteristics of educational quality will gain added attention with the expansion of the Malcolm Baldrige National Quality Award to include an award for excellence in education. In 1994, comments on the award criteria were received and an education pilot program is currently under way. The "education pilot criteria" are founded on eleven core values and concepts, which fall into a seven-part framework. This framework contains twenty-eight basic, interrelated, results-oriented requirements. These criteria are "directed toward improved overall school performance results . . . [and] focus principally on five key areas of school performance . . . (1) student performance, (2) student success/satisfaction, (3) stakeholder satisfaction, (4) school performance relative to comparable schools, (5) effective and efficient use of resources. Improvements in these five results area contribute to overall school performance" (National Institute of Standards and Technology, 1994, p. 10). As the Baldrige Award develops and specific measures of performance are established, the college publishers who rate and rank colleges will need to take notice.

Conclusion

The effort to find a model of undergraduate quality is difficult, though there may be common characteristics of quality apparent to many. As Boyer (1987, p. 287) concluded, "There is no single model of 'the good college.' Missions and circumstances vary greatly from one campus to another. But there are, we believe, characteristics widely enough shared."

The search for these widely accepted characteristics is the challenge for the future. Pascarella and Terenzini (1991, p. 596) believe such a search needs a change in direction, away from its current focus on resource wealth and more toward those aspects of student life that have important effects on outcomes: "such factors as curricular experiences and course work patterns, the quality of teaching, the frequency and focus of student-faculty nonclassroom interaction, the nature of peer group and extracurricular activities, and the extent to which institutional structures and policies facilitate student academic and social involvement."

With all the effort to quantify quality, there is a subjective aspect of higher education and student development that cannot be collected and analyzed. A statement in Salem College's 1994 admissions literature may best sum up these realities: "Choosing a college is a chance to choose who you will be. If you choose a college that pushes and encourages you, your mind will grow in power and strength. If you choose a college that listens to you, you will learn to speak with assurance and clarity. If you choose a college that believes in you, you will come to believe in yourself."

The search for predictors of student-environment fit and characteristics of educational quality, whether quantitative or qualitative, will continue. This search should not turn administrators into Navin Johnsons shouting "the new phone books are here." It is the responsibility of institutional research professionals and magazine publishers to continue to work toward methodologies that are founded on sound constructs and are presented to the public in an appropriate manner. Failure to meet this responsibility will only reinforce the myopic drive-by and sound bite mentality on which many Americans depend when they examine important issues. The diversity within higher education institutions and prospective students demands that simplistic quality models without adequate explanations of their shortcomings be replaced by more robust and fully explained models developed in conjunction with the higher education community.

BRUCE I. MALLETTE is assistant provost for administration at North Carolina State University, Raleigh. He is a member of the Association for Institutional Research's Higher Education Data Policy Committee, former president of the North Carolina Association for Institutional Research, and former member of the executive committee of the Southern Association for Institutional Research.

*Validity criteria can and should be applied to reputational study
models, and research that tests their validity and reliability should
be conducted. Such concerns, while weighing heavily on the minds
of institutional researchers and others on campus, have typically not
been raised by consumers and publishers. Two studies of* U.S. News
& World Report's *"America's Best Colleges" suggest that this guide's
validity may be suspect and that systematic research and development
are long overdue.*

Validity Issues for Reputational Studies

Michael D. McGuire

The growth in the number and prominence of reputational studies of American colleges and universities in recent years might best be understood as the confluence of at least two factors. First, increases in the published costs and decreases in the selectivity of many institutions have paradoxically made them both more and less accessible to the average college-bound high school senior. This situation has been further complicated by the widespread growth of tuition discounting and educational loans, which have brought net short-term costs of higher education down to affordable levels for many students and their families. Discounting and selectivity have an interactive effect at many private institutions: Deeper discounts are offered to higher achieving students, while lower achievers who can afford to pay for their own education are often offered admission but little or no tuition discount at institutions that would have rejected them outright in the past. The effect of these phenomena is widespread chaos, bordering on panic, in the admissions marketplace of the 1990s.

Second, colleges and universities have responded to this heightened competitiveness with massive and often grandiose self-promotion campaigns. The average high school junior or senior (or, increasingly, sophomore) is now bombarded with an unprecedented number of unsolicited viewbooks, catalogues, videos, letters, and telephone calls from prospective institutions; the situation is even worse for the above-average student. These promotional materials are obviously biased, each promising more educational riches and personal fulfillment than the next. The effect of this media blitz is information overload, with both the quantity and subjectivity of the sales pitches adding to the consumer's sense of confusion and helplessness.

Within such a context of market mayhem, it is not surprising that consumers will seek out information sources that can provide an objective third-party point of view, simplify the overwhelming complex college selection

NEW DIRECTIONS FOR INSTITUTIONAL RESEARCH, no. 88, Winter 1995 © Jossey-Bass Publishers process, and provide some comparative sense of institutional quality. College guidebooks and reputational studies supply the first of these services; only reputational studies, with their emphasis on statistical summaries and rank orderings, tend to supply the others. Nor is it surprising that reputational studies are especially popular in this age of statistical obsession and an all-but-incomprehensible higher education marketplace, where the need for simplification and quantification is most acute.

One of the most important issues of reputational studies involves the validity of their rankings and the methodologies used to develop them. This is obviously a concern for the institutions being compared, since invalid rankings can unfairly damage their reputations and undermine their competitiveness. Less obvious is the concern that consumers should feel: College choice is a crucial and far-reaching life decision, and if it is based on misleading information, it is the student who ultimately suffers the most. Questions of validity are seldom raised by consumers, however, who place blind trust in the objectivity and integrity of the reputational study publishers without examining the methodological underpinnings of the rankings. This trust may even be fueled by their distrust of and disgust with the institutions that bombard them with self-promotional materials.

Central to the validity of reputational studies is the definition of quality. If one can rank America's "best colleges" or "best buys," then by definition one must have operationalized quality and value. The fact that a given reputational study is marketed to consumers with very different needs, talents, ambitions, and pocketbooks, however, suggests that a unitary definition of quality or value is an oversimplification of an inescapably complicated and personal decision. What is best for one student may not be even close to best for another.

Types of Validity

There are many types of validity that are applicable to various measurements. Three of obvious concern to reputational studies are face validity, construct validity, and predictive validity.

Face Validity. Face validity refers to whether a method of measurement "looks valid" to those being measured, to those performing the measurement, and, perhaps most important, to those who use the resulting information (Anastasi, 1988). Face validity is the least technical type of validity, dealing not with what a ranking system actually measures but with what it appears superficially to measure. As Anastasi (1988, p. 144) noted, "Fundamentally, the question of face validity concerns rapport and public relations." The face validity of reputational study methodologies is linked to the consumer confusion and promotional overload described above and is reinforced by traditional stereotypes and hierarchies in higher education. The American public seems to believe—indeed, needs to believe—that some colleges and universities are better than others, and that the manner in which they are better can be quantified. The ordinal rankings that comprise reputational studies are accepted unquestioningly by the public because they seem intuitively sensible; in fact, ordinal rankings are a pervasive facet of our culture and there is no reason to believe that higher education can or should be exempt from this scorecard mentality.

Construct Validity. Striking closer to the heart of the education community's unease over rankings, construct validity is the extent to which a ranking system may be said to measure a theoretical construct, in this case, education quality. How quality is defined and measured by a ranking system can be gleaned from the variables and weights used to determine the rankings. For example, in the 1994 edition of *U.S. News & World Report*'s "America's Best Colleges," rankings are derived from seventeen subfactors clustered among six categories: academic reputation, student selectivity, faculty resources, graduation rate, financial resources, and alumni satisfaction. One of the major criticisms of this methodology is the fact that the measures used to define quality are relatively far removed from the tangible educational experiences of students.

For example, in what ways does the average compensation of full professors at a college (one of the variables in the faculty resources dimension) impart qualitative differences in the average student's undergraduate experience? If one accepts as true every link in a rather circuitous daisy chain of cause and effect—that well-paid faculty are better teachers and mentors than poorly paid faculty, that faculty are rewarded financially for good teaching, that institutions that compensate their full professors well are more successful in recruiting the best and the brightest to their faculties, and that somehow all of this trickles down to superior face-to-face encounters and classroom and mentoring experiences at high-salary versus low-salary institutions—then construct validity can be implied if not demonstrated. At best, however, this is indirect evidence substituting for direct evidence for the simple reason that no one has been able to define and operationalize educational quality to the degree necessary to measure it reliably. In the absence of good measures, poor measures will have to suffice because the consumer demand for some type of measurement is strong and the business of supplying that demand is lucrative.

Predictive Validity. A third type of validity, predictive validity, follows closely on the heels of construct validity. If in fact one institution has greater "educational quality" than another, the outcomes of having attended a higher-quality institution will be more favorable than those of having attended a lower-quality institution. The simplistic notion of comparing institutions on a variety of "outcome" measures—placement rates in jobs and graduate or professional schools, later-life satisfaction, higher salaries, and other achievements—quickly becomes murky when one considers the virtual impossibility of controlling for various student characteristics, or input measures. If the graduates of college A are more successful in life than the graduates of college B, can college A justifiably take credit for the difference? In particular, institutions that attract students from privileged backgrounds will almost always be able to demonstrate superior postgraduate outcomes even if the quality of the undergraduate experience was mediocre.

Astin (1992), among others, has argued for an appropriately multidimensional approach in promoting his I-E-O (inputs-environment-outputs) model. Measuring and controlling for student inputs is at best a crude endeavor for the same reason that specifying the quality of the undergraduate environment is—we simply do not have adequate measures. The kinds of statistical quality controls that are available to manufacturing are not, and probably never will be, available to those in the field of education.

In summary, the validity of reputational studies has been implied and wished for but never thoroughly demonstrated. Ironically, the American public has not demanded the same degree of accountability from reputational study publishers as it has of standardized test publishers. The latter spend tens of millions of dollars annually in exhaustive research and development to satisfy those higher standards; it is no coincidence that the cost of taking the Scholastic Aptitude Test (SAT) or Graduate Record Examination is many times the cover price of "America's Best Colleges."

Research on Validity: A Case Study

The general validity concerns described above can be illustrated by examining the results of research done on the validity of one reputational study, *U.S. News'* "America's Best Colleges." While some of the issues raised by this research are specific to "America's Best Colleges," many are applicable to other studies that attempt to create a single quantitative index of educational quality or value and to rank colleges and universities on that index (see Mallette, this volume, for broader discussion of and references on these topics).

The *U.S. News* model is complex. In the "America's Best Colleges" guide published in the fall of 1994, rankings were based on institutions' relative performance in six major ranking categories, which were in turn composed of seventeen weighted subfactors (see Table 5.1). Categories, subfactors, and weights vary from year to year, and at least some weights and subfactors vary between the college and university groups or between national and regional groups. The research described below was based on the "America's Best Colleges" guide published in the fall of 1992; changes in methodology between 1992 and 1994 are noted as appropriate. To avoid confusion, only the method used to rank the national liberal arts colleges is discussed below, although the same concerns can be expected to apply to other institutional categories.

Academic Reputation. This category is based on the results of a survey of college presidents, academic deans, and admissions directors conducted by *U.S. News & World Report*. The 1994 survey achieved a record response rate of 66 percent. Respondents rank institutions within their own institutions' group (national universities, national liberal arts colleges, regional colleges and universities, and so on) by quartile; these rankings are collapsed into a single rank for each institution. Academic reputation accounted for 25 percent of the final ranking in both 1992 and 1994. Critics of this category cite the low response rate on the *U.S. News* survey, the undetermined representativeness of the respondent group, the

Table 5.1. Rank and Influence of *U.S. News & World Report's* Factors and Subfactors

Factor (Percentage Weight in Total Score)	Subfactor	Subfactor Percentage Weight in Total Score	Rank of Weight in Score
Academic reputation (25%)	Reputation survey	25.00	1
Student selectivity (25%)	Acceptance rate (accepted/applied)	3.75	10
	Yield rate (enrolled/accepted)	2.50	11
	Percentage in top 10% of high school class	10.00[a]	3
	Percentage in top 25% of high school class	10.00[b]	3
	Average or midpoint score on SAT/ACT scores	8.75	4
Faculty resources (20%)	Average compensation: all ranks	7.00	6 tie
	Percentage of full-time faculty with doctorates or other terminal degrees	7.00	6 tie
	Full-time faculty as percentage of total faculty	4.00	9
	Student-faculty ratio	1.00	13
	Percentage of undergraduate classes with		
	1–9 students	0.40	14
	10–19 students	0.20	15 tie
	50–99 students	0.20	15 tie
	100 or more students	0.20	15 tie
Graduation rate (15%)	Six-year graduation rate for last four first-year cohorts	15.00	2
Financial resources (10%)	Education expenditures per student	8.00	5
	Other education and general expenditures per student	2.00	12
Alumni satisfaction (5%)	Average percentage of living alumni, excluding those with graduate degrees, who gave in the past two years	5.00	8

Note: The Subfactor Percentage Weight column expresses the contribution or weight of each subfactor to the total score. Those weights are then ranked in the rightmost column. For example, acceptance rate is a subfactor under student selectivity; acceptance rate is weighted 15 percent within student selectivity, which is in turn weighted 25 percent toward the total score; that means that the acceptance rate is weighted 15 percent x 25 percent = 3.75 percent toward the total score and is thus ranked tenth among all the subfactors in its contribution to the total score. SAT = Scholastic Aptitude Test, ACT = American College Test.

[a]National universities and liberal arts colleges.

[b]Regional colleges and universities, including liberal arts colleges.

obvious and probably self-serving biases among respondents, the ambiguity of "reputation" as a construct, and the excessive weight carried by this category in the final rankings especially given its questionable validity.

Student Selectivity. This category, which accounted for 25 percent of the final ranking, is based on four weighted subfactors: first-year acceptance rate (20 percent of this category in 1992 and 15 percent in 1994), yield or matriculation rate (weighted 10 percent in 1992 and 1994), percentage of first-year students who graduated in the top 10 percent of their high school classes (weighted 35 percent in 1992 and 40 percent in 1994), and average SAT/ American College Test (ACT) scores (weighted 35 percent in 1992 and 1994). These data are self-reported by participating colleges and universities. Critics of this category cite its overreliance on broad market characteristics (acceptance rate and yield) that penalize institutions with nonmainstream missions and focused admissions strategies, and its emphasis on the academic profile of incoming students rather than on how well each institution maximizes the potential of the students it matriculates. High school class rank is also difficult to interpret without information on the quality of the high schools themselves, and the much-publicized limitations of the SAT and ACT (and the often suspect ways in which institutions self-report those scores) suggest that their high weights may not be justified from a validity standpoint.

Faculty Resources. This category, which accounted for 20 percent of the final ranking, was based on five weighted subfactors in 1994: average faculty compensation (weighted 30 percent in 1992 and 35 percent in 1994), percentage of full-time faculty with terminal degrees (weighted 30 percent in 1992 and 35 percent in 1994), percentage of faculty with part-time status (weighted 20 percent in 1992 and 1994), student-to-faculty ratio (weighted 20 percent in 1992 and 5 percent in 1994), and average undergraduate class size (weighted 5 percent in 1994). The 1992 rankings did not include the average class size subfactor, and the average faculty compensation was based on full professors only rather than on all ranks as in 1994. These data are self-reported by participating colleges and universities. Critics of this category cite its emphasis on institutional wealth and the implied causal relationship between wealth and instructional quality. Ignored in the formula are the actual classroom and out-of-classroom experiences that form the very substance of an undergraduate education.

Graduation Rate. This category accounted for 15 percent of the final ranking in 1994, up from 10 percent in 1992. It consists of the averaged six-year graduation rates of the four most recent student cohorts (a five-year graduation rate was used in 1992). These data are self-reported by participating colleges and universities. Critics of this category argue that high graduation rates can be a function of incoming student characteristics, low academic standards, or both, rather than educational quality. Colleges that take fewer at-risk students or that have less rigorous curricula and completion standards would be expected to have higher graduation rates than colleges with larger numbers of at-risk students and more rigorous academic standards.

Financial Resources. This category accounted for 10 percent of the final ranking in 1994, down from 15 percent in 1992. There are two subfactors: educational expenditures per student (weighted 80 percent both years) and other expenditures per student (weighted 20 percent both years). These data are self-reported by participating colleges and universities. Critics of this category cite its emphasis on wealth and murky spending patterns rather than on fiscal efficiency and educational substance. The implication that high spending produces better learning does not appear to have empirical backing (Pascarella and Terenzini, 1991). One might even argue that the emphasis on expenditures encourages an escalation of costs and tuition in higher education, a trend that has incurred its full share of public wrath in recent years.

Alumni Satisfaction. This category accounted for 5 percent of the final ranking in 1992 and 1994. It was based on a two-year average of the percentage of a school's living alumni who gave to the institution's fundraising drives. These data are self-reported by participating colleges and universities. Critics question the validity of alumni giving rates as a measure of satisfaction: Giving may be a function of alumni ability to give (which in turn may be related to career choice or family background), or an institution's aggressiveness and resulting effectiveness in soliciting funds, rather than satisfaction per se.

Validity: Four Overarching Issues

Four major concerns are evident in the methodology reviewed above. First, all of the data are self-reported by institutions, which have a clear and strong motivation to present themselves in the best light possible. The brisk sales of "America's Best Colleges" have caught the reluctant attention of even the most hardened critic, and the temptation to respond creatively to the *U.S. News* survey—especially to the more ambiguous questions, and especially by the institutions that have the most to gain or lose from the rankings—is undeniable. Inaccurate data, whether submitted accidentally or intentionally, undermine the fundamental validity of the rankings. It is not currently possible to estimate the degree of measurement error produced by incorrect data.

Second, frequent changes in the specific subfactors and their weights make year-to-year shifts in rankings difficult to interpret and even more difficult to explain to audiences both on and off campus. While efforts of *U.S. News* to improve its methodology are laudable, the resulting incomparability of the model over time is a source of major confusion and dismay on many campuses. As the research described below demonstrates, even small changes in weights can produce significant changes in the final rankings—the bottom line of "America's Best Colleges" and similar publications.

Third, the choice of categories, subfactors, and weights in "America's Best Colleges" is arbitrary and based on convenience and intuition rather than research. The editors of "America's Best Colleges" acknowledge that better measures of educational quality simply do not yet exist, and in all probability never will. In the absence of true measures, available proxies are substituted. A heavy reliance on resource subfactors without first demonstrating a relationship between resources and educational quality is an aggravating feature of the model. While this may be the only realistic solution given the state of the art in measurement (other than not performing rankings at all, which would kill the golden goose that "America's Best Colleges" is for *U.S. News*), it speaks around rather than to the issue of validity. At the very least, using empirically derived weights, such as those yielded in the study described below, would improve the validity of the model.

Fourth, given the various validity concerns outlined in this volume, one would hope for some warning to consumers not to overinterpret the rankings. The "America's Best Colleges" published in 1994 includes an expanded design and methodology section that improves somewhat on past editions. Unfortunately, like most warning labels, those pages understate the severity of the danger and probably tend to be overlooked by most consumers. One would also expect more blatant disclaimers to have a dampening effect on sales of "America's Best Colleges."

Research on the *U.S. News* Model

"America's Best Colleges" provides an excellent laboratory for testing at least some of the validity concerns that critics have raised with respect to its specific methodology and to the notion of empirical rankings of colleges and universities in general. I conducted two studies on this topic in 1992–1993. The first study addressed the issue of the arbitrariness of the "America's Best Colleges" weights, and the second examined the sensitivity of the final rankings to relatively minor fluctuations in those weights. To the extent that consumers are inclined to use "America's Best Colleges" to perform at least an initial screening in the college selection process, the integrity and stability of those rankings should be as thoroughly established as possible (see Webster, 1992b, for a somewhat different critique of "America's Best Colleges"). Research can be a valuable tool to accomplish this goal.

Study 1: Arbitrariness of *U.S. News* Weights. In my first study, I attempted to determine the degree to which the "America's Best Colleges" weights chosen arbitrarily by the editors of *U.S. News* corresponded with those from a panel of higher education "experts"—the same college presidents, academic deans, and admissions directors who received the "America's Best Colleges" reputational survey. In the summer of 1992, a questionnaire asking respondents to supply optimal weights for the "America's Best Colleges" model was sent to the presidents, academic deans, and admissions directors of fifty-five national liberal arts colleges that were members of the Higher Education Data Sharing (HEDS) consortium. Participants received the following instruction: "Even if you do not agree that these are necessarily the best variables for defining educational quality, please assign weights to indicate the relative importance of each one." They were also asked to suggest alternative measures of educational quality for possible inclusion in future versions of "America's Best Colleges." The study was not performed by *U.S. News,* although the magazine's director of data analysis was informed about the study and he provided me with corollary data.

The participation rate in this survey was encouraging, especially when compared to the modest response rate of the "America's Best Colleges" reputational survey: 129 of the 165 administrators surveyed (78 percent) returned a completed questionnaire. Presidents (82 percent) were more likely to participate than were academic deans (73 percent), perhaps reflecting their heightened interest in marketing issues generally, and in forging improvements in the validity of the *U.S. News* methodology specifically.

The results of this study reveal both areas of agreement and areas of disagreement between the panel of experts surveyed and the editors of *U.S. News.* These findings are summarized in Table 5.2. Within each of the major categories, the largest disagreements in subfactor weights were noted for student-faculty ratio (weighted much more heavily by the experts than by *U.S. News*), average faculty compensation (weighted much more heavily by *U.S. News* than by the experts), high school class rank and yield (weighted somewhat more heavily by the experts than by *U.S. News*), and average SAT/ACT scores (weighted somewhat more heavily by *U.S. News* than by the experts).

One interpretation of these data is that higher education insiders recognize the student-faculty ratio, in spite of its limitations, as a subfactor that attempts to measure the quality of the interaction between students and faculty. The significant lowering of the weight for this subfactor in 1994 is therefore disheartening. A second observation is that higher education insiders appear to recognize the inferior predictive validity of SAT and ACT scores compared to high school academic performance, a finding repeatedly uncovered in validity studies of standardized admissions tests (Shepard, 1984).

Among the major categories that comprise the final ranking, faculty resources and financial resources were weighted somewhat more heavily by the experts than by *U.S. News,* and reputation was weighted much more heavily by *U.S. News* than by the experts. This latter finding is ironic indeed, since the experts in this survey (as a group) were the same ones who completed the reputational survey that provided *U.S. News* with its reputational data! A lesser irony is that the expert would have increased the weight given to faculty resources and financial resources, yet in the open-ended comments section some criticized the "America's Best Colleges" model for emphasizing wealth over educational processes.

In the final analysis, there may be no "best weights" for use in the "America's Best Colleges" study. While the panel of experts in the study described above disagreed on average with *U.S. News* in some significant ways, they also disagreed among themselves with regularity. The point of this research was not to designate optimal weights but rather to suggest that empirically derived weights are better than arbitrarily chosen ones and that research on the topic can and should be done. If the effort that *U.S. News* expends to sell advertising in its publications were devoted to refining the "America's Best Colleges" methodology, the validity of the product could be substantially higher.

Table 5.2. Subfactor Weights Assigned by Panel Versus U.S. News

	Selectivity				Retention			Faculty Resources	Student/		Overall Score				
	Top 10 Percent	Acceptance Percentage	SAT/ACT Scores	Yield	Alumni Dollars	Graduation Percentage	Part-Time Percentage	Ph.D. Percentage	Faculty Ratio	Faculty Compensation	Selectivity	Faculty Resources	Financial Resources	Retention	Reputation
Admissions Directors															
Mean	43	17	26	14	16	45	10	22	30	12	25	25	19	20	12
Standard deviation	18	14	12	12	14	17	7	8	12	8	11	8	7	11	8
Academic Deans															
Mean	39	14	29	18	23	43	11	20	30	14	20	28	22	17	13
Standard deviation	11	8	11	11	13	14	8	9	10	9	7	9	10	6	7
Presidents															
Mean	41	14	30	15	23	44	14	20	28	15	21	25	21	20	13
Standard deviation	14	11	11	10	15	18	11	11	9	10	8	6	7	10	8
All Respondents															
Unweighted mean	41	15	29	16	32	68	15	28	39	18	22	26	21	19	13
Standard deviation	14	11	12	11	14	16	9	9	10	9	9	8	8	8	8
1992 U.S. News Weights	35	20	35	10	33	67	20	30	20	30	25	20	15	15	25
Difference in standard deviations	−6	5	6	−6	1	−1	5	2	−19	12	3	−6	−6	−4	12
	−0.42	0.50	0.56	−0.53	0.07	−0.06	0.54	0.27	−1.80	1.29	0.36	−0.74	−0.68	−0.42	1.60

Study 2: Sensitivity of Rankings to Changes in Weights. As both a practical and a conceptual matter, the vulnerability of the "America's Best Colleges" rankings to shifts as a result of minor changes in weights (or, in theory, the subfactors themselves) is a critical issue worthy of investigation. If the model is relatively stable, then disagreements about the value of different weights become trivial. If, on the other hand, institutions change rank and even quartile when weights change, the danger of misrepresenting institutions to the public increases significantly. The fact that the *U.S. News* weights were not determined empirically also becomes a damning weakness in the study design.

Institutional data from the 1992 "America's Best Colleges" study were provided to me by *U.S. News* to test the sensitivity of the rankings. The 140 national liberal arts colleges were reranked using three alternative weighting schemes: (1) the average weights suggested by the panel of experts (see above), (2) those weights varied by one-half a standard deviation (some weights increased, some weights decreased, so they added to 100 percent within a category or within the final ranking), and (3) those weights varied by one-half a standard deviation in the opposite direction (so every subfactor was increased or decreased in each scheme). The purpose of these variations was to create, in the absence of "industry standards," different sets of reasonable weights: The experts' proposed weights were deemed inherently reasonable, and deviations of only one-half a standard deviation seemed well within the bounds of reason (by definition, the central tendencies of the panel of experts were captured within that proximity to the mean). Since any given set of weights might be no more valid or stable than the set used by *U.S. News*, multiple schemes were tested. A composite of the differences in rankings derived from the three alternative weighting schemes was computed as well, to summarize the findings.

When the national liberal arts colleges were reranked using these other weights, shifts in ranks were readily apparent (see Table 5.3). Specifically, 88 percent of the colleges on average changed rank under the alternative schemes. Some institutions improved in rank by as many as twenty-four places; others declined in rank by as many as twenty-two places (the average shift was approximately five places). As one might expect, the greatest amount of movement was noted around the middle of the distribution (second and third quartiles), although even among the elite top twenty-five, 77 percent of the colleges changed rank by as many as five places.

Of greater concern to most institutions than changes in specific rank were changes in quartile. *U.S. News* does not yet publish specific ranks for all institutions; beyond the top twenty-five, all others are grouped by quartile. In terms of representation to the readership of "America's Best Colleges," the quartile is usually the most relevant level of aggregation. Results of the sensitivity analysis reveal that a significant number of institutions (although fewer than changed rank) also changed quartile under the alternative weighting schemes. Specifically, an average of twenty-one colleges (15 percent) were ranked in a different quartile under the alternative schemes compared to the *U.S. News* weights and rankings. Equal numbers of institutions improved and declined, suggesting that any changes in weights will produce a ratings windfall and consequent exuberance for some

Table 5.3. Change in Ranking Based on Changes in Weights

Model 1 Quartile	N	Changed Rank N Changing	Percentage	Mean Shift in Rank	Largest Upshift	Largest Downshift	Changed Quartile N Changing	Direction
Top 25	25	20	.80	1.52	5	−4	1	down
Rest of first 10	10	9	.90	3.40	8	−10	3	1 up, 2 down
Second	35˘	33	.94	6.20	15	−15	6	2 up, 4 down
Third	35	30	.86	5.37	24	−16	6	4 up, 2 down
Fourth	35	28	.80	3.83	15	−15	2	up
Total	140	120	.86	4.36	24	−16	18	
Percentage of total							.13	
Model 2								
Top 25	25	18	.72	1.16	4	−3	1	down
Rest of first 10	10	8	.80	3.00	9	−8	3	1 up, 2 down
Second	35˘	32	.91	6.14	9	−22	7	2 up, 5 down
Third	35	35	1.00	6.66	24	−17	8	5 up, 3 down
Fourth	35	30	.86	5.20	24	−22	3	up
Total	140	123	.88	4.92	24	−22	22	
Percentage of total							.16	
Model 3								
Top 25	25	20	.80	1.76	5	−5	1	down
Rest of first 10	10	9	.90	4.50	8	−10	3	1 up, 2 down
Second	35˘	33	.94	7.17	21	−21	8	2 up, 6 down
Third	35	32	.91	5.37	22	−19	9	6 up, 3 down
Fourth	35	31	.89	3.97	13	−7	3	up
Total	140	125	.89	4.76	22	−21	24	
Percentage of total							.17	
Composite								
Top 25	25	19	.77	1.48	5	−5	1	down
Rest of first 10	10	9	.87	3.63	9	−10	3	1 up, 2 down
Second	35˘	33	.93	6.50	21	−22	7	2 up, 5 down
Third	35	32	.92	5.80	24	−19	8	5 up, 3 down
Fourth	35	30	.85	4.33	24	−22	3	up
Total	140	123	.88	4.68	24	−22	21	
Percentage of total							.15	

institutions and a ratings deficit and dismay for others. This observation high-lights an important consideration in revising the "America's Best Colleges" model: Some institutions will fare less well in the rankings under an "improved" system.

In summary, these results indicate that weights do matter, and that changes in weights produce changes in rankings independently of any changes in the institutions ranked. This suggests that a rational rather than arbitrary weighting scheme should be implemented, and that year-to-year changes in weights should be minimized. The lack of comparability of rankings across time under a fluid methodology is not mentioned by the authors of "America's Best Colleges," yet it is clear that various constituencies track colleges' rank-ings over time and inaccurately interpret changes as evidence of institutional progress or decline.

Validity Revisited

Earlier in this chapter, three types of validity—face, construct, and predictive—were discussed. The premise that measurement tools need to demonstrate acceptable levels of those, and perhaps other, types of validity was set forth. In light of the research findings presented here, let us now reexamine the three types of validity and search for evidence of them in "America's Best Colleges."

The face validity of "America's Best Colleges" is probably its strong suit: The belief that colleges and universities do differ on various quality dimensions is widespread, and it follows that those differences should be measurable and comparable. Certainly the popularity of *Consumer Reports* attests the public's predisposition to "comparison shopping," using as a guide an objective third party's research-driven evaluations of competing products or service providers. Why should higher education be immune to this societal phenomenon?

Where the validity argument begins to break down for "America's Best Colleges" is in the area of construct validity. Two sidebars are worthy of note: First, in this 228-page publication, with its massive readership and market influence, fewer than 3 pages are devoted to methodological issues (the methodology itself is described in 1 page). Second, this scant coverage of the foundation on which the publication stands is actually an expansion of previ-ous years' methodology sections.

If the construct in question is quality (which the title "America's Best Col-leges" suggests rather pointedly), what is the evidence that the measures within the model capture differences in quality and that the method for weighting those measures and compiling the rankings preserve those quality differences? The authors of "America's Best Colleges" admit that the evidence is largely cir-cumstantial and intuitive: Institutions that are judged subjectively by their peers to be better, that spend more money on their faculty and their educa-tional programs, that matriculate students with better academic credentials and reject larger numbers of applicants, and that graduate students faster and are more successful in raising money from alumni are "better" than institutions with lesser track records in those areas. By their own admission, the authors of "America's Best Colleges" do not have access to *direct* measures of academic quality because those measures do not yet exist in common, comparable formats: "Unfortunately, no one has yet developed a reliable and practical system of measuring outcomes" ("America's Best Colleges: 1995 Annual Guide," 1994, p. 5). This shortcoming in the state of the measurement arts does not de facto validate the "America's Best Colleges" method, however.

As far as the method for weighting those measures and compiling the rankings is concerned, the scant research on the topic fails to provide evidence of validity. On the contrary, the two studies described above suggest that the arbitrary weights used by *U.S. News* differ in minor to major ways from those offered by a panel of experts, and that the impact of even minor differences can be significant on resulting rankings. These problems call into question the construct validity of the rankings themselves, and the integrity of "America's Best Colleges."

In many ways, predictive validity is at the heart of the consumer interest in "America's Best Colleges." Prospective students and their families read guidebooks and reputational studies in an effort to predict their own futures—their future success and happiness while, and after, attending a given institution of higher learning. To the extent that higher-ranked institutions offer a higher probability of success and happiness than lower-ranked institutions, "America's Best Colleges" has demonstrated predictive validity. Unfortunately, the subfactors in this guide have little or nothing to do with the success and happiness of students and alumni. On the contrary, the vast majority of those subfactors are measures of institutional wealth and selectivity, which are highly correlated with one another but probably not at all correlated with any meaningful educational outcome once student input measures have been factored out (see Astin, 1992; Pascarella and Terenzini, 1991, for a full discussion of these issues). America's best colleges are in essence America's most prestigious colleges, according to *U.S. News*, and that association does a grave disservice to those less-prestigious institutions that build a solid life foundation for their students using fewer resources and more modest student inputs.

Conclusion and Possible Futures

It seems appropriate to conclude this chapter with a return to the issue of what colleges and universities are attempting to sell to the American public, and how reputational studies attempt to portray differences among the myriad institutions competing for the nation's students. How one conceptualizes the "product" of American higher education seems like a straightforward question, but further analysis suggests that the answer can range from "knowledge and skills" to "an intense but often sheltered middle-class socialization experience," to "a credential with market value." In fact, the correct answer is "all of the above." The product of our colleges and universities is multifaceted, and the means by which that product is delivered varies enormously from one place to another.

Given this overwhelming complexity of substance and variety of delivery mechanisms, and the unique talents and needs and ambitions and expectations of the millions of students enrolling in the thousands of colleges and universities every year, how can a single metric accurately capture this diversity and place a useful value on it for the consumer? Ordinal scales of quality or value are by definition unidimensional and reductionistic; the phenomena they are attempting to measure are multidimensional and complex. This consideration does not argue against the publication of reputational studies per se, and in any event such an argument would be futile given the public's strong attraction to them. What it does argue against is the derivation of a single number, with highly questionable validity and reliability, that somehow magically encapsulates the worth of different institutions and then makes value judgments about those institutions based on that number.

Finally, the issue of continuing research in the field of reputational studies merits the attention and cooperation of the publishers, the public, and the colleges and universities alike. The focus of future work should include the educational processes that occur at different institutions and the educational (and other life) outcomes that result. Perhaps the survey of college presidents, deans, and admissions directors that *U.S. News* conducts every year should be expanded to include other participants. How do alumni and employers define educational quality? An investment in higher education has lifelong repercussions, and both those who have received that education and those who manage the postgraduate workplace should have much to contribute to the debate.

Such data would address that aspect of construct validity known as convergent validation: A valid measure should correlate highly with other measures with which it should theoretically correlate (Anastasi, 1988, p. 156). Such evidence would lend powerful support to the validity of reputational studies, enhancing their appeal to consumers and strengthening them in the eyes of the academy.

MICHAEL D. MCGUIRE *is director of research for the Pennsylvania Independent College and University Research Center and chair of the Association for Institutional Research Higher Education Data Policy Committee. He is former president of the North East Association for Institutional Research and former executive director of the Higher Education Data Sharing Consortium.*

In recent years, colleges and universities have been flooded by surveys from publishers of college guides and from popular newsstand magazines. This chapter describes the response of the higher education community to the burden of these surveys and, in particular, the standard survey response currently being used by the University of California at Berkeley.

Managing the Information Overload: The Case for a Standard Survey Response

Anne Machung

Sheron Quigley (1992) nicely captures the dilemma addressed in this chapter:

> As assistant to the associate provost of university enrollment, I am often the person who assembles the responses to surveys about Northwestern University. I realize that most of these surveys, taken singly, are helpful and informative: but when they seem to come in battalions, they can be overwhelming for the person trying to complete the forms. One day, after filling in hundreds of little boxes with numbers and percentages, I vented my feelings by drafting a possible counterattack:
>
> Dear Survey Publisher:
>
> Each year we are asked to provide, at no cost, information on a community of some 20,000 scholars to people who intend to make a profit from our contribution. We are delighted to perform this service; however, as collecting and organizing the information runs to about $5,000 worth of time and research on the part of our university officers and staff, we have instituted the following scale of charges:

Stuff you could find out by looking in the view book	$10.00 per answer
Stuff you could find out by looking in the newspaper	$5.00 per answer
Stuff which we would have to be crazy to tell you	No Sale
Stuff we must fabricate in order to provide (Note: there is an additional charge for legal costs should a lawsuit result)	$200.00 per answer
Stuff which is nobody's business anyway	$400.00 per answer

Stuff which would take an inordinate amount	
of rooting around for to no one's benefit	$500.00 per answer
Stuff which nobody even cares about except	
it gives you a different angle for your book	$650.00 per answer

I know that people like you, who are dedicated to providing quality information for the youth of America, will understand that these are only token charges to offset the increasing costs of serving the informationally challenged. We are not asking (at least, not yet) for a percentage of the profits from the sale of your guide. We are seeking only to break even on the enterprise.

For your convenience, we have marked the 250 questions you sent us according to category. On the attached order blank, please indicate which answer you wish to purchase and return the sheet with your remittance. We will rush your completed survey to you by return mail.

Sincerely
The Admissions Office

Dilemma of Responding to College Guidebook Surveys

In recent years, colleges and universities have been flooded by surveys from publishers of college guides and from popular newsstand magazines like *U.S. News & World Report* and *Money Magazine,* which rate institutions for "quality of undergraduate education" or "best buy." Schools have responded to these surveys out of concern they would be misrepresented (or, worse yet, not represented at all) in various publications—and hence might lose some potentially good publicity and potentially good students. Publishers, in turn, have fed into and helped produce this anxiety by claiming that there is "no change for this service" and that it is in each school's "best interest" to respond. But is it really in each school's best interest to respond, and is the service that publishers provide really so free of charge?

Across the country college administrators have become increasingly distressed at the amount of time and effort that answering each survey individually requires. The questionnaires are often quite lengthy and detailed. Frequently, they are mutually redundant, asking for similar types of information but in slightly different ways. For example, the *Wintergreen/Orchard House Survey Form for 1993–94* (1993, p. 4) requests the percentage of entering first-year students whose verbal and math Scholastic Aptitude Test (SAT) scores fall within one of six different intervals, while the *College Entrance Examination Board Annual Survey of Colleges, 1994–95* (1994, p. 15) requests the actual verbal and math SAT scores of entering first-year students at the twenty-fifth and seventy-fifth percentiles. While such differences may seem trivial, ferreting these differences out is extremely tedious and time-consuming.

Cost of Responding to Surveys. Answering these surveys requires extensive coordination across campus offices and sometimes new data collection and programming efforts. For example, in their 1994 college ranking survey, *U.S.*

News asked for the number of students enrolled in different sizes of graduate and undergraduate classes. Not a particularly difficult question to answer, except that *U.S. News* defined an undergraduate course as any course in which an undergraduate was enrolled and a graduate course as any course in which a graduate student was enrolled. Not only was this definition in itself idiosyncratic since no campus defines undergraduate and graduate level courses by random patterns of student enrollment, but answering it on the Berkeley campus in the way *U.S. News* requested required several extra hours of special programming.

Conservatively, I estimate that responding to these surveys costs the University of California (UC) at Berkeley at least one full-time equivalent (FTE) per year. At $40,000 per FTE, this amounts to a subsidy of $40 million per year from colleges and universities to the college guidebook publishing industry. While this may seem like a high estimate to some, answering the scores of college guidebook and rating surveys every year involves both staff and coordination of staff across multiple offices on campus: public relations, institutional and student research, admissions, financial aid, accounting, and housing, to name the most prominent. Even assuming this effort costs a campus only one-quarter FTE per year, one is still talking about a subsidy of $10 million per year. Moreover, these estimates are based on the assumption that publishers receive about one thousand returned surveys. In all probability, this is a low estimate. According to the Carnegie Foundation, there are 1,400 four-year colleges and universities in the United States today. Assuming a response rate of about 90 percent, which is what College Entrance Examination Board and Wintergreen/Orchard House claim to get, about 1,260 four-year colleges respond to college guidebooks surveys. Using this higher figure generates an information subsidy between $12.6 and $50.4 million, assuming each school spends somewhere between .25 and 1.0 FTE answering surveys each year. Moreover, this estimate does not take into account what the nation's 1,480 two-year colleges spend answering college guidebook surveys.

Commercial Use of Data Collected from Colleges. While the manifest purpose of college guidebook surveys is to collect information for college guidebooks, much of the information collected is not published in college guidebooks at all. Rather, it is used for other purposes, such as developing large data bases, some of which are sold commercially. A major part of the profit involved in collecting information from colleges and universities comes from selling that information back to private corporations, government agencies, and even colleges and universities themselves. For example, in 1994 Wintergreen/Orchard House sold a data base to Hewlett-Packard, which used it to develop computer products for the college market. Peterson's, an editor there told me, regularly sells its data bases to insurance companies. And, though company officials later changed their minds, in 1994 *U.S. News* offered to sell back to colleges and universities the data base it had originally collected from them free of charge.

Proliferation of Surveys. The number, length, and amount of information requested is growing. In 1993, for example, Peterson's sent seven different surveys to UC Berkeley. Its survey of graduate programs alone was 140 pages long. That same year *U.S. News & World Report* added a whole new set of questions about financial aid to its standard survey of undergraduate institutions. In fact, the *U.S. News* survey has grown from a single question—"What schools would you recommend for your own children?"—asked of college presidents in 1983, to a 14-page questionnaire that in 1995 required extensive coordination across offices to answer.

Impact of Technology. The widespread availability of information technology is propelling this quest for more information. Indeed, the market for college guidebooks is rapidly proliferating. There are college guidebooks for students with learning disabilities and those with high SAT scores. There are specialized texts for minority students, transfer students, foreign students, and Christian students. Clearly, the college guidebook market is a profitable one. Costs are relatively low in part because colleges and universities supply most of the information free of charge. But they are also low because new information technologies allow publishers to combine and recombine data from different surveys in all sorts of specialized ways and sell that information to different market segments in a multitude of different formats (books, magazines, CD-ROMs, computerized software programs, and so on).

However, new information technology is not totally to blame. Colleges and universities fuel this process by treating surveys very seriously and responding to them on an immediate and ongoing basis. Schools feel dependent on college guidebooks for outreach and publicity. Staff fear that not responding to these surveys could hurt recruitment efforts. They also fear retaliation from publishers—letters or telephone calls to their presidents or chancellors complaining about surveys not answered, published information that is incorrect, zeros substituted for missing data. But the ultimate downside to this process is that the more information schools provide, the more publishers request. Indeed, some publishers have even come to feel that higher education institutions owe them information free of charge. For example, Martin Nemko (1993) invited 250 institutions to participate in his *College Matchmaker* guidebook project, to be published by Little, Brown. Distinguishing *College Matchmaker* from other college guidebooks was Nemko's request that institutions randomly survey 250–300 undergraduates at their own expense. When a number of institutions balked at doing so—"basically, we're doing this fellow's research for him," said one—Nemko withdrew the project, but not without blaming institutions for planning to "cheat" on his survey.

Higher Education Community Responds

Responding to this deluge of requests for information, in 1992 the Association of American Universities Data Exchange established a subcommittee to examine the feasibility of developing a standard instrument to use when responding to college guide surveys. Panels at the Association for Institutional Research (AIR) forums in 1993 and 1994 also discussed the burden increasingly placed on college and university offices by college guidebook surveys. The Higher

Education Data Policy Committee of AIR, the public relations group of the Association of American Universities, the American Association of Collegiate Registrars and Admissions Officers (AACRAO), and the National Association of College Admissions Counselors are all interested in developing some kind of common survey instrument.

The main idea behind a common instrument is that instead of responding to particular sets of questions sent by dozens of publishers of college guides, colleges and universities can send the same set of information to all inquirers. Doing so would significantly reduce the burden that individually answering each survey places on a single institution. Preparing one comprehensive response obviously is much more efficient than responding to dozens of similar, but slightly different, questionnaires. The point is not to withhold information from publishers but to provide them with what they need in a format that is convenient for colleges and universities.

The exact form this instrument will take is still under discussion. Two formats have been suggested: an institutionally specific model versus a single universal survey with common definitions. Both have advantages and disadvantages, but using either one would enormously reduce the burden college guidebook surveys place on campuses.

Berkeley Prototype

Drawing primarily from information actually published in college guidebooks, I have developed an institutionally specific prototype for UC Berkeley. The prototype consists of two documents: a standard survey response for UC Berkeley and a publication list. The standard survey response provides basic information on the campus (for example, enrollment, faculty size, admissions policies, and library holdings) and includes only items that are common to several surveys and published in the guidebooks, and that are of actual value to parents and students prospecting for colleges. The publications list outlines a set of standard campus publications and national data collection reports, such as the National Center for Education Statistics Integrated Postsecondary Education Data System (IPEDS), that provide more detailed information on various programs and issues. In 1995 both the chancellor of UC Berkeley and the vice chancellor's advisory council endorsed this prototype. Beginning in fall 1995, the Berkeley campus will provide this basic set of information, along with a complimentary copy of the *General Catalog,* to all college guide publishers upon request. (Copies of Berkeley's standard survey response are available from the Office of Planning and Analysis, Chancellor's Office-Budget and Planning, 200 California Hall, University of California at Berkeley, Berkeley, CA 94720-1510.)

Rationale. In developing Berkeley's prototype, I analyzed surveys from Barron's, College Entrance Examination Board, College Counsel, Chronicle College Databooks, Wintergreen/Orchard House, and Peterson's. I also reviewed each of the leading college guidebooks that they publish and compared what they asked in their surveys to what they published. Publishers claim they need different surveys because they are publishing guidebooks for different segments of the market. However, while there is a significant amount of variety in the kinds of information that publishers request, I found that there is remarkable similarity in what they publish. Admittedly, there is some variety; some guidebooks include interviews with students, others pride themselves on a particular attribute, like Barron's "Index of Selectivity," but in general the standard guidebooks are more alike than they are different. This should not be surprising. Just as Honda, Toyota, and GEO Metro compete for different portions of the small-car market, so Peterson's, the College Entrance Examination Board, and Wintergreen/Orchard House compete for different portions of the college guidebook market. Like the automobile market, the college guidebook market also is segmented into general bookstores and reference markets, and into general guidebooks, regional guidebooks, and specialized guidebooks. Just as single publishers put out guidebooks for different segments of the college guidebook market, so within segments of that market they compete with one another for larger portions. How else to explain all the general bookstore guides on the market that seem remarkably similar to one another?

Advantages. The strength of the Berkeley prototype is that it outlines all the standard information a prospective student typically would want to know about a campus. Indeed, the Berkeley prototype was designed with this criterion in mind: The information provided to college guidebook publishers should be useful to prospective students and their parents. Second, the Berkeley prototype relies on existing campus data and publications. It does not require institutional research or admissions offices to engage in additional data collection. Third, it is easy to design and easy to implement, requiring only campuswide approval, not the endorsement of many institutions. Last, it eliminates the cost of providing information not published in college guidebooks. By adopting the Berkeley prototype and adapting it for their own use, colleges and universities can continue to be represented in major college guides without getting caught up in providing information, free of charge, for the proliferating market of specialized guidebooks and computer software products of profit-making corporations.

Limitations. There are limitations to Berkeley's standard survey response, as there are for any piece of standard information. The major limitation of this approach is that publishers do not receive all the information they request in exactly the format they want. Some (especially those with short one- or two-page questionnaires) get more information than they request, others get less. Excluded are such esoteric data as the minimum grade for which credit is awarded for each advanced placement examination in Latin (Virgil) as opposed to Latin (Literature), or the type of management software used for admissions and records information (*College Entrance Examination Board Annual Survey of Colleges, 1994–95,* 1994, pp. 8–9, 23). Obviously, information like this is irrelevant to prospective first-year students, their parents, and high school admissions counselors. Included, however, is information on enrollments, accreditation, admissions policies, tuition and fees, academic programs, graduation rates, campus housing, social, cultural, and athletic activities, special programs for physically disabled or learning disabled students, health services on campus, and career planning and placement services.

Most, if not all, surveying organizations now request an enormous amount of information, most of it in their own individualized, precoded, machine-readable formats. By providing exactly what is requested in the formats requested, colleges and universities have significantly reduced the cost of publishing college guidebooks. However, adopting a standard survey response like the Berkeley prototype would require publishers to sift through the information provided and code it themselves. In essence, this would shift the burden of research costs from colleges and universities (who for years have been subsidizing the publishing industry) back onto the publishers themselves. But this is my point: Campuses can no longer continue to subsidize these industries, especially as their requests for information escalate while our resource bases shrink.

Single Standard Survey Instrument

An alternative approach to an institutionally specific model like the Berkeley prototype is a single standard survey instrument using universally agreed on definitions for all variables. Like the Berkeley prototype, a single standard survey would reduce the burden of answering multiple surveys, but unlike the Berkeley prototype it would present information in the same format using common definitions. Such a survey would create a uniform data set of very high quality, which is one of its main attractions. It would also be much easier for publishers to extract information common to several schools from a single standard survey than from an institutionally specific model. In fact, Arthur Rothkopf, president of Lafayette College, has recommended that college administrators take the lead and work with authors and editors of the major rankings to develop a standard form for reporting important statistics (Rothkopf, 1995).

Problems with a Standard Survey. While intuitively appealing, a single standard survey approach immediately generates very difficult questions. Which reporting statistics to use? Who should develop them, colleges and universities or publishers? Given the diversity in higher education institutions, can enough common statistics be developed to satisfy both publishers and schools? And will schools, anxious to put their best feet forward, be willing to report data using common definitions that could put them in an unflattering light vis-à-vis their competitors?

The task of constructing unambiguous definitions that simultaneously fit a large number of different types of institutions, ranging from two-year vocational colleges to large, research-oriented, multicampus multiversities, is daunting. Take tuition as an example. Some schools, like the Massachusetts Institute of Technology, charge everybody, graduate and undergraduate alike, a flat rate per year. Other schools, like UC Berkeley, charge "fees" but not "tuition"; however, many of these fees, like the university registration fee, educational fee, and Berkeley campus fee, look suspiciously like tuition. Other schools, like the University of Michigan at Ann Arbor, have extraordinarily complicated fee structures that vary by level of student, date of admittance, major, and so on. And still other schools simply charge on a per credit basis—so much for so many credits. Obviously, even a seemingly simple question such as "How much tuition do you charge?" can produce an array of complicated answers. Multiply the number of definitions needed to answer a single question by the number of questions asked in a standard survey and one has produced an overwhelmingly complicated and confusing document.

Moreover, schools disagree, both in practice and in principle, over how to count and measure basic statistics. Even seemingly innocuous variables, such as the number of applications received, the number of seniors graduating, or the number of teaching faculty, raise thorny political issues. The academic reputation of a school, for example, depends at least partially on its selectivity. Presumably, the more selective the school, the better the quality of undergraduates and faculty it attracts. Selectivity is defined in part by the ratio of number of students admitted to number applied: Harvard admits one out of seventeen students, California State University at Fresno admits almost nine out of ten. However, counting half-completed applications or even telephone inquiries as applications can raise the tally of total applications received and thus raise a school's selectivity ratio. While changes in the definition of "number of applications received" probably would not affect Harvard or Stanford greatly, they could—and do—affect less well known schools that are striving to attract better-quality students (for an excellent discussion of these issues, see Knowlton, 1995). Issues about how to count applications, how to track cohorts of graduating seniors, and how to count faculty are thus highly contested. If colleges and universities cannot agree on how to measure one variable like graduation rates, as debates around the Student Right-to-Know Act indicate, how can they be expected to agree on one hundred common definitions in a standard survey instrument? And if they cannot agree on the definitions, will they actually use that instrument once developed?

In 1983 a committee of AACRAO, chaired by Stan Henderson, developed a standardized college profile report form for responding to college guidebook surveys. Despite the effort put into developing this instrument, only a few schools used it. The instrument never took off, in part because it requested data in too simplified a format and in part because it was never publicized enough.

Advantages of Ambiguity. Publishers' solutions to the enormous complexity and diversity among higher education institutions has been to keep it simple: Let most definitions remain ambiguous and let each institution determine how it wants to define itself. While this solution may offend those who have been trained in the canons of objective scientific research, it is important to recognize that such ambiguity serves not just publishers' needs but institutional interests as well.

The same data, for example, are often used for different ends, and these ends can be at cross-purposes. For example, the institutional researcher's goal of producing high-quality data for comparative purposes can conflict with the public relations officer's desire to present the institution in the best possible light. The former wants clear, consistent, unambiguous definitions; the latter goes for loose, flexible, and ambiguous definitions. The conflict produced by using data for different ends shows up in many different ways. If one wants to plan the curriculum in a department for the coming year, for example, one needs to know exactly how many faculty will be available for teaching. However, if one wishes to construct a student-faculty ratio that will attract students, perhaps it is better to count faculty on sabbatical leave, faculty with research appointments, visiting faculty, part-time faculty, adjunct faculty, and possibly even emeriti faculty since presumably these will be available to students at some point in their academic careers.

Clear definitions are most possible, and most likely to be used, when the information requested is straightforward, relatively easy to collect, and not politically sensitive. Enrollment figures and degree programs are cases in point, hence the easy availability of IPEDS definitions. However, when data become more difficult to collect and more politically sensitive, establishing consensually agreed on definitions, as debates over Student Right-to-Know demonstrate, is far more complicated. Indeed, these are the shoals on which a common survey instrument has floundered to date.

Issues to Consider in Designing and Adopting a Standard Survey Instrument

How much of the information published is actually reaching those it is designed to teach—potential undergraduates, their parents, and high school and college admissions officers? This is difficult to answer. Publishers cite circulation figures, but in themselves circulation figures say little about how college guidebooks and software programs are actually used. Clearly, college guidebooks do sell, otherwise they would not be published. And undergraduates do look at them. However, how many undergraduates make their decisions on which college to attend on such a rational basis as this?

Moreover, how many high school admissions counselors consult college guidebooks? Most of the information here is anecdotal and impressionistic. Visiting local high schools, one college admissions counselor found only a few schools in her part of Texas had bought any of the standardized guidebooks or computerized software packages now on the market. Budgets were limited, and in some cases schools did not have computers large enough to handle the data sets. Those who had purchased computerized software programs did not allow students to use them. But this varies. Almost all the high school guidance counselors in Maryland whom Huntington and Ochsner (1993, pp. 55–59) surveyed used a variety of college guidebooks, though only a few had used any of the software packages on the market.

How helpful are college guidebooks to entering first-year students? The answer to this is murky as well. However, it seems that college guidebooks are indeed sources of information students use when prospecting for colleges. The College of Wooster, for example, found that most of their incoming first-year students in the fall of 1990 had consulted at least one college guidebook, and often more than one; at the same time many of these students felt that "the guides ought to be a supplement to, rather than a substitute for, campus visits or gathering information directly from colleges" (Nicholson, 1991, p. 29). Carleton College found that 30 percent of its incoming first-year class in September 1991 had looked at college guidebooks before deciding on Carleton. At the University of Maryland at College Park more than one-quarter of new students surveyed in the summer of 1992 had used either *The College Handbook* or "America's Best Colleges" and found them useful in deciding to attend Maryland (Huntington and Ochsner, 1993, pp. 55–59). Likewise, a 1993 survey at Rutgers found that 35 to 45 percent of entering first-year students considered college guidebooks either important or very important in helping them select Rutgers. Not clear from all of this survey evidence, however, was how these students actually used college guidebooks and how those who did not use guidebooks made their decisions.

What impact might adopting a standard survey response have on a school's outreach and recruitment efforts? This is an area of great concern and anxiety, especially for public relations personnel, but whether their concerns are justified is simply not known. Admittedly, many colleges and universities consider college guidebooks an important marketing device, but how much schools benefit from the publicity that college guidebooks provide is by no means clear. Would admissions applications, for example, decline if schools were not represented in college guidebooks? Most probably, this varies by type of institution, size, and academic reputation. Larger, more prestigious schools, such as UC Berkeley, Harvard, and Yale, depend less on college guidebooks for attracting students than smaller, less well known institutions. Berkeley, for example, depends mostly on its academic reputation for attracting students. Its problem is not one of attracting a sufficient number of qualified undergraduates but rather of justifying admissions turndowns to those who are also highly qualified. In solving this problem, college guidebooks are of little help. But smaller private schools, like Mills, John Masters College, and Occidental College in California, that depend on college guidebooks for attracting students often do not have sufficient resources for answering college guidebook surveys. Their institutional research offices often consist of only one person who simply does not have the time to answer each college guidebook survey. Ironically, smaller schools that most need the publicity offered by college guidebooks may have the fewest resources for providing publishers the information they request.

How will publishers respond to a package of standard information? This is a big concern on campuses, especially among those looking for balance between satisfying publishers' requests for information and institutional needs for reducing workload. Increasingly, a number of publishers recognize the burden that answering surveys places on university administrations, and some, like Peterson's and Wintergreen/Orchard House, are receptive to the idea of a common survey instrument. Wintergreen/Orchard House, for example, has given some institutions permission to answer other survey requests with their survey, in effect using the Wintergreen/Orchard House instrument as a standard survey. There are a number of problems, however, connected with using the Wintergreen/Orchard House instrument as a standardized instrument. For one, colleges and universities do not want to be put into the position of favoring one publisher over another. Second, the Wintergreen/Orchard House instrument also includes items, such as the total number of microcomputers on campus or the percentage of graduates who enter the job market in a field related to their majors within two years of graduation, that are very difficult, if not impossible, to answer short of highly expensive student surveys. Peterson's and *U.S. News* now incorporate IPEDS definitions into their surveys. While using standard definitions, like IPEDS enrollment data, does help to simplify the reporting requirement, IPEDS alone is totally insufficient because 80 to 90 percent of the information requested by most surveys is not covered by IPEDS, or indeed by any other national survey instrument. While these efforts are commendable, publishers' advice and feedback will be invaluable as schools develop a more comprehensive survey instrument. To reach a mutually agreeable format, university administrators and college guidebook publishers need to cooperate with each other.

How should schools handle the many specialized requests for information they receive? Typically, specialized surveys—on graduate programs, financial aid, or programs for minority, disabled, transfer, or foreign students—ask highly detailed questions, most of which cannot be answered by a standard undergraduate survey. On an individual basis schools might choose to answer some specialized surveys, such as surveys about specific graduate programs, while still using a standard survey response for answering general questions about their undergraduate programs.

How should schools handle ranking surveys sent out by major news organizations such as U.S. News & World Report *and* Money Magazine? This is a very sensitive issue given the publicity that accompanies nationally advertised ratings, and some higher education institutions may want to continue answering rating surveys on an individual basis. However, a policy of answering college guidebook surveys with a standard survey instrument while answering rating surveys on an individual basis could give rating magazines license to request virtually anything they want from colleges and universities and expect to receive it. In turn, this approach would allow major news magazines to develop huge data bases replete with information about higher education while denying a similar commercial opportunity to college guidebook publishers. It could also force college guidebook publishers into the rating game themselves in an attempt to keep open the flow of information to them. One solution is to limit the amount of information provided to magazines like *U.S. News & World Report* and *Money Magazine* to only those variables they actually use when developing their ratings.

What about the future? As I have argued throughout this chapter, the number of surveys, their length, and the amount of information requested will continue to grow as information technology becomes cheaper and easier to use. Wintergreen/Orchard House, Peterson's, and the College Entrance Examination Board already produce slightly different versions of the same book for what they claim are different segments of the market but in reality are probably different portions of the same market segment. To ask a basic question, How necessary is all this information? One of the basic assumptions of the information age in which we now live is that the more information we have, the better off we are. But is this always true?

Obviously, students, parents, and high school admissions counselors need information in order to make good decisions about which colleges to attend. But too much information can be confusing, lead to information overload, and hinder rather than help good decision making. Rather than mindlessly adding questions to questionnaires to see what comes back, or mindlessly filling in blanks just because they are there, we should begin to identify the real information needs and to provide for those real needs. Just as there is danger in too little information, there is danger in too much—the danger that on the leveling ground of massive computerized data bases, we may lose our intuition, our sense of priorities, and our good judgment.

ANNE MACHUNG *is senior policy analyst at the University of California at Berkeley. She is currently chairing a subgroup of the Association of American Universities Data Exchange, which, in cooperation with the Association for Institutional Research, is developing a standard survey response for schools to use nationally.*

College guidebook publishers have come under great scrutiny as the number of such publications has increased. The burden of survey response is felt by the institutions who are called upon to fulfill various requests for information, often involving a number of formats. In this chapter, four major publishers of college guidebooks respond to the issues raised in the previous chapters.

Publishers' Perspectives: Guidebooks

Kimberly J. Hoeritz, Allan B. Corderman, Max Reed, Edward B. Fiske

Peterson's (Hoeritz)

Peterson's Guides, now in its thirtieth year, is the leading provider of college guidebook and educational reference material. Nicholson (1991, pp. 24, 29) has highlighted *Peterson's Guide to Four-Year Colleges* as "[carrying] on a tradition of excellent reporting of basic information" and judged it as the "most accurate" guide. It is not by chance that Peterson's has earned a reputation as an excellent resource for those seeking information about postsecondary opportunities.

Throughout its history, Peterson's mission has remained constant: bringing individuals and institutions together and providing the best information for decision making while giving institutions a responsible communications channel to serve their very real information outreach needs. The Research Division is careful in its data collection efforts, and Peterson's as a whole has kept in touch with higher education issues, changes, and consumer information needs. Consistent with its commitment to higher education, Peterson's shares concerns raised by the higher education community regarding the proliferation of surveys and the integrity of data reporting, and the company wishes to work toward a good resolution of these issues. All interested parties have the same ultimate goals: to preserve the free flow of information and ideas, to serve all users of education information, and to relieve unreasonable burdens on the information providers. We at Peterson's are confident that these goals can be met.

Peterson's Foundation. *Peterson's Guide to Graduate Programs* was first published in 1966, and *Peterson's Guide to Four-Year Colleges* appeared for the first time in 1970. These guides were created through carefully developed surveys, innovative questions, and a seriousness of purpose. As objective data sources, the guides were intended to provide factual and comparative information that prospective students and parents could utilize as they researched colleges and universities. The original 1966 edition of the *Annual Guide to Graduate Study* was the first organized resource on graduate study in the United States and Canada. The disciplinary organization was the first to allow variously named programs and departments to be classified into an accepted structure with a standard taxonomy. The undergraduate guide was the first to provide new kinds of data about each college drawn from original research and to present textual information supplied by colleges themselves.

Credibility is key with Peterson's Guides, for over the years the data collection and presentation methods have been standardized, and Peterson's has not engaged in subjective, narrative, or evaluative reporting on colleges. In fact, a point that has been made and is represented in this volume is that the intent and use of college guides like Peterson's are significantly different from the intent and use of guides that rate or rank. We would like to see all professionals, including the National Association of College Admission Counselors (NACAC) in its *Guide to College Guidebooks,* make this distinction and its implications clearer to students. At the same time, Peterson's has always followed the role recommended by NACAC in regard to publishers' responsibilities: "The publisher is responsible for making the publication as inclusive, accurate, and responsibly devised as possible" (NACAC, 1994, p. 57). From the beginning, it was understood that Peterson's is working with and on behalf of the academic community, providing educators with a central forum that is acceptable to them as a means of organized, dependable outreach to new generations of students. The organization and objectivity of the guides are as important to the academic community as they are vital to the needs of readers—a dual mission Peterson's serves to this day.

Today's Issues. Two facts are evident: The number of publications serving educational choice is growing and the demand for them exists. The growth in the overall number of publications, services, and corresponding surveys has resulted from an increased need for accurate and specific information on the part of families and guidance professionals to assist them in the college selection process. It is well recognized that today's students and parents evaluate schools and programs more discriminatingly, and Peterson's provides a needed service for both families and colleges by offering a timely, trustworthy, and international flow of good information. While it may be true that little research exists on the effect of guidebooks on the college selection process, it was reported in one survey of high school students that 59 percent had used at least one college guide in their college search (Boyer, 1988, p. 3). These same students grouped guidebook usage together with college representatives, high school counselors, and college mailings as resources utilized in the college selection process. College guidebooks continue to serve a vital and ongoing reference need, as an initial information source and constant fact-check during the application process.

This heightened interest from information users and the subsequent response of publishers have resulted in an increased demand on the data providers. Peterson's is prepared to work with the institutions and professional associations on ways to make the demand for information more reasonable and manageable. In April and May 1995, Peterson's representatives attended the American Association of Collegiate Registrars and Admission Officers and the Association for Institutional Research (AIR) conferences to meet face-to-face with those feeling the impact of survey issues and to identify ways in which solutions could be reached. As a result of those meetings, Peterson's has volunteered to participate in discussions on two issues of particular importance: the development and implementation of a standard core-data survey instrument and data definitions. It is understood that resources are being limited or eliminated across colleges and universities affecting an institution's ability to respond to growing requests for data. As the demand for college guidebooks will not go away, nor will the need for higher education research data, a better method for collecting the data that addresses the concerns of data providers and meets the needs of users must be developed. What must also be reconciled is a publisher's natural interest in new ways of inquiry against a data provider's normal wish for a minimal, consistent survey instrument.

Standard Core-Data Survey. In an attempt to standardize the data collection effort, some institutions have developed a standard survey response, while the professional associations are discussing the development of a standard data collection instrument. Peterson's favors a standard survey instrument, covering core-data elements, rather than a standard response report for a very important reason: The standard response supplies a limited amount of information about an institution. The University of California at Berkeley's standard survey response (see Machung, this volume) was evaluated against the Peterson's annual survey of undergraduate institutions, and the data collection effort resulted in the loss of detailed information regarding many student activities and services, computer and research facilities, financial aid, and academic and graduate requirements. What makes Peterson's publications so useful is the level of detail reported and the ability for institutions to respond with specific answers to open-ended questions. This richness will be lost for schools that return a standard response in lieu of completing the survey because the uniquely addressed attributes of the academic and cultural environments will not be represented. With this in mind, Peterson's proposes that a standard survey covering a core-data set be created, leaving serious publishers free to append important unique questions.

Data Integrity and Validity. It is clear that in order for our varied data users to best utilize our data resources and research efforts, they must be able to compare like information. A common set of data definitions not only eliminates the confusion often felt by survey respondents as well as those reading the resulting publications but also makes the data more meaningful in that they can be compared among reports and across institutions in an appropriate context. Moreover, it is important that data presented in publications on which students and parents rely for accurate and meaningful information be representative of higher education's academic and administrative structures and reflect the way institutions view themselves. Having carefully constructed survey items for decades, Peterson's, in recognizing the importance of common data definitions, wishes to participate in discussions involving their adoption.

Peterson's is extremely sensitive to other reporting issues such as the validity of data. In peak seasons, the Research Division at Peterson's employs over sixty-five editors and analysts who work specifically on editing and verifying the survey data received from colleges and universities. Telephone calls are made to survey respondents for missing or discrepant data or to verify figures that may have changed significantly from the previous year. Once the data are keyed into the data base, proof-prints are generated and compared against the original survey to ensure that the correct information was keyed. Once all keying is complete, logical error checks are run against the data base, over thirteen hundred checks for the undergraduate data base alone, and all free text is printed in the form of text-read reports so that data consistency can be evaluated. Certain sensitive data, such as accreditation and National Collegiate Athletic Association graduation rates, are collected from those administrative bodies and incorporated into institutional records.

To ensure accurate interpretation by the survey respondent as well as the reader, Peterson's provides data definitions with its surveys. These definitions are incorporated in the front matter of publications so readers understand what it is they are being presented with. All data reported by institutions and verified are printed in the guides. Data are presented consistently across institutional profiles, so descriptions are comparable, and a response rate in excess of 90 percent for the undergraduate and graduate survey efforts yields comprehensive, useful information for readers and researchers, both in a given year and on a longitudinal basis.

Peterson's does not impose a ranking or rating system in its data collection or reporting. As evidenced by numerous reports, articles, and analyses of methodology, rankings and ratings have no validity because true measures of academic quality do not exist. In Peterson's Guide to Four-Year Colleges, institutions are asked to evaluate their own levels of entrance difficulty so that prospective students can assess their chances for admission based on each profile of the previous year's entering class. These levels are not intended as measures of quality. Terenzini and Pascarella (1994) report that traditional measures of quality have an inconsistent and "trivial" correlation with how much students grow or change. Astin (1992) reports that faculty, student, and peer group interaction will have more of an impact on a student's educational experience than the type of institution one attends. Furthermore, student performance and outcome measures have been identified as more a reflection of the student than of the institution attended (Terenzini and Pascarella, 1994). Peterson's strives to keep its data collection and reporting as objective and consistent as possible, realizing that a best fit for a student is a delicate combination of academic, cultural, and personal attributes.

Cooperating with Data Providers. To ease survey response, Peterson's is developing plans to support electronic transfer of surveys either via e-mail or on disk. Feedback from survey respondents also indicates that verification of survey responses may also take place through e-mail. In this way, our inquiries are less intrusive, and respondents may return messages at their convenience. In preparation for the second edition of *Strategic Indicators for Higher Education,* published in conjunction with the Association of Governing Boards, the survey instrument has been modified so that, when available, the Integrated Postsecondary Education Data System (IPEDS) equivalent response has been identified next to the Peterson's question. Adopting more standards, particularly IPEDS as recommended by members of AIR, will allow Peterson's survey instruments to be completed in a more efficient manner. We are also putting systems into place that will allow dynamic update of institutional data, creating data resources that are as current as users want or need.

As a publisher, Peterson's has responsibilities to its data providers (the institutions) and to its constituents (students and researchers). To further those ends, Peterson's aims to participate with the professional organizations representing the interests of data providers to evaluate the data collection effort. In developing a standard core-data survey instrument, focusing this aspect of data collection on the most common needs and uses of the data, and taking advantage of electronic transfer when possible, the information community can provide a great service for all of its members. Normalizing the data and data definitions and presenting the results in an objective manner will facilitate their use and enhance their quality. Peterson's looks forward to working toward these ends.

Wintergreen/Orchard House (Corderman)

Most of the other chapters in this volume address the activities of publishers involved in producing college guidebooks sold in the consumer market (Barron's, College Entrance Examination Board, Lovejoy's, Peterson's, and others) and those involved in publishing college ratings guides (*Money Magazine* and *U.S. News & World Report*). However, there has been no mention of the activities and needs of the equally important (although not as large) segment of college guidebook and college search software publishing represented by firms such as Wintergreen/Orchard House, College View, and Careerware-Choices. These firms are devoted to publishing college information in the depth and breadth needed by professional counselors at the high school and community college level who work with students on planning their future career objectives and identifying their educational needs. Although a great many of these students are well qualified for admission to the colleges of their choice, many others are special talent and special case students, marginal students, and special needs students who must find unique situations of college offerings and requirements. These counselors and students are best served by college guidebooks and software packages that are much more sophisticated, more accurate, more complete, and more up-to-date than the consumer guidebooks and ratings publications. This kind of in-depth information also facilitates tens of thousands of counselors' efforts in sorting out students in their pre-application stages so they will only apply to colleges where they have a reasonable chance of success. This results in major savings to the colleges as well as the students and their parents. Families making first-time applications are especially in need of this type of professional counseling.

College Admissions Data Service Handbook. The professional market segment was carved out by Educational Research Corporation (ERC), a nonprofit organization established and operated by the faculty of Harvard University's Graduate School of Education. ERC was established in 1938 to conduct broad-ranged studies on the effectiveness of various educational practices and programs. In the 1950s the staff of ERC became concerned that the newly emerging cadre of professional school-based guidance counselors had inadequate basic information about four-year colleges to be effective in counseling college-bound students. At the time only *Lovejoy's College Guide* (first published in 1940) and a few other similar publications were available, and they only listed very basic information about the colleges. In the interest of filling this information gap, ERC embarked on an ambitious research, design, and publishing program that culminated in the debut of the *College Admissions Data Service Handbook* (*CADS*), a two-volume guidebook that offers two pages of very specific college admissions information on each of several hundred liberal arts colleges. Although this publication was not widely promoted at the time, it gained instant recognition as *the* college admissions data source among high school counselors, particularly among those in the Northeast. By including other four-year accredited colleges and developing an extensive index of majors and sports, *CADS* was expanded over the next thirty-five years into three volumes, then four volumes, and, finally, into a five-volume set of over 3,960 pages describing more than 1,660 institutions. In 1978 ERC sold the rights to *CADS* and its data base to Orchard House, Inc., of Concord, Massachusetts. Orchard House continued to broaden and expand *CADS,* changed the publication's name to the *College Admissions Data Handbook,* computerized its data into a fully relational data base, and added two-year colleges, graduate schools, technical and proprietary schools, and private scholarships to the data base. Orchard House also started selling college and scholarship data to other selected publishers of professional guidebooks and software products for the professional and consumer markets. Less than 1 percent of the firm's college data sales are to organizations using the data for noneducational product or service applications. In 1993 Orchard House moved its headquarters to New Orleans, Louisiana, and in 1994 merged with Wintergreen Software, a leading educational software publisher, to form Wintergreen/Orchard House (WOH).

Professional Market's Special Need for College and Scholarship Data. The professional market consists primarily of college advisers and guidance and career counselors working with students in planning their careers and postsecondary education. It also includes reference librarians serving the same population segments. These types of counselors can be found in both public and private secondary schools, community colleges, and in private practice.

Other chapters in this volume focus on guidebooks and ratings publications that have been developed for the consumer market—primarily students and their parents. Surveys of users of these types of publications frequently find that "they were of little use in selecting the colleges of their choice," and other, similar surveys often find that "the advice of guidance counselors and teachers was of significant importance." It is from up-to-date and accurate professional publications and software that many of these teachers and counselors receive their basic information, and in the depth that they need it. It is impossible for such advisers to know all they need to know about the thousands of college options available to the youth of today by referring to the relatively narrowly based and shallow consumer-type guidebooks on the market today. And many of the other better-known consumer guidebooks are only compiled every two or three years and are, therefore, very out-of-date for serious use by professionals working with students planning for admission to college in the near future. The ratings guides, although interesting, are woefully short on details about admissions criteria, procedures, deadline dates, advanced placement and early decision policies, and the myriad other, similar detailed information needs of professional counselors. It is just this area of need that the professional publishers concentrate on in designing and compiling their products.

Another recent trend in the design of data-gathering instruments and the actual gathering of data for use by publishers in developing products for the professional market is that these tasks are being done primarily by one firm, WOH. This has come about primarily because WOH has more experience than any other firm in the field, they have the largest and most accurate data base available, and their charges to participating publishers are modest and far less than it would cost the publishers to develop the data themselves. WOH is currently providing data for fourteen college guidebooks and sixteen different college and scholarship search software programs. The guidebooks include *Lovejoy's College Guide,* Arco's *The Right College,* Princeton Review's publications, and many others. The software programs include College View, American College Test's (ACT's) Discover program, Careerware's Choices program, *Money's* "College Finder," and numerous others. Also, WOH is the primary college data supplier to *Money Magazine* for its annual *Money Guide: Your Best College Buys Now* and also supplies college data to *U.S. News & World Report* for use in various products for the consumer market.

The advantage to all of these participating publishers is that they can count on a very high response rate because of WOH's excellent reputation with college data providers and a high-quality job of collecting and collating the data by a highly experienced data base team who concentrate on nothing else all year long. This expertise allows these publishers to focus all of their energies on developing useful, high-quality products and services without wasting valuable time and resources on the extremely difficult job of gathering and collating basic college data. In a similar fashion, the advantage to the college data providers with this approach is that they are now supplying data to over thirty-two different products and services provided by a large number of publishers via a single broad-based standardized questionnaire. In spite of the fact that data providers are still inundated with data requests from large numbers of requesters, largely unknown, WOH's data-gathering role is saving them untold hours of additional research and response time.

Publishers' Role in Reducing the Burden on Data Providers. The major data compilers have been active in recent AIR forums devoted to exploring the problems institutional researchers have in keeping up with the proliferation of requests for data from publishers in the face of staff cutbacks and growing internal demands for additional information. Some of these AIR forums and also the AIR Higher Education Data Policy Committee meetings have touched on the concept of all colleges and universities coming up with some form of standardized data "template" or standardized instrument for reporting relevant measurable and quantifiable data relating to college admissions—one that all colleges can and will adopt.

Throughout all of this discussion, the responsible major publishers and data compilers have indicated that they want to be part of the solution, not part of the problem, a position that I endorse as a publisher and as an AIR forum panel participant. The only request that we, the publishers (and particularly the publishers of products and services serving the professional market), want to make is that our legitimate needs for data not be ignored or "legislated out." We are willing to ask only for data that are needed for specific products and services and that, in fact, actually appear in the products. And we are willing to be very specific as to why each data element is needed and for which constituency.

The major data base compilers would like to serve actively on any association committees that are defining such standardized instruments. Several of us are active AIR members and we have a lot of experience to contribute in solving this major problem, which affects us all. We are truly partners in the overall educational process. Although most of us are profit-making concerns (technically, if not actually!), we believe that we contribute substantially to the dissemination of accurate, complete, and up-to-date information to prospective college students on a cost-effective basis. Just as Anne Machung (this volume) has argued that the colleges are contributing up to $50 million in free data-gathering services to the publishing industry, the publishing industry can rightfully make a similar claim that we are contributing at least as much in free data dissemination services, saving the colleges millions in marketing, design, printing, and postage costs.

With respect to relieving the "crunch" on institutional researchers who are burdened with data requests from publishers on top of the growing demands from within their universities, it is obvious that college administrators should be made fully aware of all of the demands that are placed on institutional research (IR) staff so that they can support them accordingly. Experience has shown that when push comes to shove, the administrators (presidents, alumni relations officers, public relations directors, and so on) almost always find a way for the significant college data publishers to get the data they need for well-known products and services. It would be better for all concerned if administrators faced this situation directly and adequately funded IR up front, rather than hope that all of the work gets done somehow.

Action Plan. The ultimate solution to substantially reducing the institutional burden of providing data for publishers requires the publishers and the colleges to work together in developing a broad-based standardized instrument that will meet the publishers' legitimate needs for data and will be responsive to the colleges' capabilities and limitations in gathering and providing the needed data. There also has to be a way for publishers of special "niche" products to attain limited additional specialized data where this effort is in the best interests of all concerned and leads to viable products for a recognized market. At this point all that is needed to get started is for an appropriate working committee of institutional researchers and publishers to become organized and empowered, and an able leader to be appointed or elected to see the task through to a successful completion. Until this cooperative IR-publisher effort to standardize data gathering and reporting into a universally accepted format becomes a reality, the professional market data base publishers can be counted on to do their best to continue to work with institutional researchers to reduce the number of questions asked, standardize question-and-response formats, and the like. We accept the responsibility and look forward to the challenge and the opportunity to help simplify the process for all concerned.

Barron's (Reed)

As the premiere college directory that also rates colleges according to admissions standards and policies, *Barron's Profiles of American Colleges* has been the paradigm for presenting factual, helpful information to prospective college applicants. This has been possible only through the cooperation of colleges and universities in responding to Barron's biennial survey.

Anne Machung (this volume) sets forth a cogent argument in favor of a standard reporting device for reporting information to the various college directories and guidebooks—specifically, the "numbers books," as Bruce Hunter (this volume) labels them—thereby replacing the many questionnaires and surveys. Machung asks the question "How much is enough?" implying that the University of California at Berkeley's standard survey response is sufficient. Certainly, that approach addresses all of the *vital* information that the various directories try to supply. A better question, though, might be "How much does the high school student—the potential applicant—need, or want?" Where the Barron's survey strays beyond the bare-bones information on the standard survey response, it is generally an attempt to round out the portrayal of the institution.

Unlike Machung's charges toward other college guide publishers (Peterson's, College Entrance Examination Board, and Wintergreen/Orchard House), Barron's seldom requests information that is not a part of the institution's capsule or profile, or used in the selector rating computation. Further, no part of the Barron's college data base is *ever* sold commercially.

It should be noted, though, that Barron's makes a determined effort to keep survey responses on as simple a level as possible. The *Profiles* survey consists of no more than twenty-four pages, and previous responses to each question are included. Thus, the responding institution need only change the data that need updating. This generally amounts to figures that should be readily accessible: current enrollment, tuition, and financial aid data.

It should also be noted, however, that the standard survey response as presented by Machung is an adequate instrument. With the exception of the omission of standardized test score range reporting, the instrument provides for reporting the basic, fundamental information.

Hunter (this volume) presents an overview and history of the college directory and guidebook publishing scene, describing three distinct categories of the genre. I take exception, however, to his statement that the guidebooks' ratings are "nothing more than the publishers' judgments of the colleges' competitiveness for admissions." Barron's selector ratings are based on standard admissions data, quantified into a precise formula. No judgments, personal or otherwise, are a part of the selector rating process.

Additionally, it is clearly stated in *Barron's Profiles* that the selector ratings are merely a measure of the degree of difficulty in achieving acceptance to each institution. As such, the selector ratings do not encourage "narrowing [students'] focus to a small handful of 'highly ranked' institutions," as Hunter states.

Hunter refers to "so-called rankings" rather than ratings and persistently places the word *rankings* in quotation marks, thus implying a deficiency or inaccuracy in the result. The careful reader, however, will note that Barron's selector ratings are based on quantifiable data, reported by the institutions themselves.

Hossler and Foley (this volume) make the point that little is known about how and to what extent the college guidebooks are used, and they suggest that available data indicate that the directories "have small to negligible impact on most students considering colleges and universities." Countering this conclusion is the fact that the market has for many years supported, and indeed continues to support, several books of this nature.

Hossler and Foley also note the necessity for both "institutional administrators and publishers to provide timely, accurate, and useful information," a policy with which Barron's heartily concurs. Recent media attention to this issue emphasizes its importance, and guidebook publishers generally do their best to seek out, identify, and correct misinformation. Moreover, it is important that the readers of college directories understand that the computation and presentation of admission ratings are never intended as a reflection of the academic quality of a given school.

Much has been made of recent marketing efforts by colleges and universities, and thorough, accurate reporting to the various guidebooks should be a part of that effort. The popularity of the directories attests that these guidebooks are the gateway to the application process.

The Fiske Guide to Colleges (Fiske)

During the 1970s the University of Northern Kentucky (UNK) earned a minor footnote in the history of American higher education with an ingenious strategy for bolstering undergraduate enrollment. Recruiters wrote out coupons with offers of scholarships in varying amounts, purchased a substantial quantity of balloons, and put the coupons into a few "lucky balloons." The plan was to release the balloons to public fanfare in downtown Cincinnati, a prime recruiting area, and reward anyone who shagged a lucky balloon and recovered its cargo with a credit against tuition at UNK.

The balloon scheme never, shall we say, got off the ground. State officials in Frankfort ruled that airborne student assistance lacked the dignity befitting public higher education in the commonwealth of Kentucky. In addition, law enforcement officials in Cincinnati, fearful that prospective students would arm themselves with weapons suitable for bringing balloons to earth, declared the launching to be a threat to public safety. But while it became a nonevent, the plan was by no means a total failure. News of the scheme made it onto the international wire of United Press International and generated applications from international students. To this day there are people in faraway places like Sri Lanka and India who, when they think of American higher education, think of Harvard, Yale, and UNK.

I recount the UNK strategy as further evidence of what Bruce Hunter (this volume) so aptly termed the "loss of innocence" that has transformed college admissions in the United States over the last two decades. It was a deflowering that had its origins in decisions taken by colleges and universities struggling with changing demographics. By the late 1970s the bulge of baby boomers finally worked its way through the higher education snake, and college administrators who had luxuriated in constant growth throughout the post–World War II period suddenly found themselves confronting a new and disturbing problem: declining enrollment. Rather than accept downsizing, which had not yet become fashionable in management circles, their response was to attempt to maintain their enrollments through marketing. Thus was ushered in the era of glitzy viewbooks, mailings targeted by Scholastic Aptitude Test (SAT) scores and upscale zip codes, and, later, videos with electronically airbrushed portrayals of campus life.

Marketing of Higher Education. As education editor of the *New York Times* during this period, I observed this movement from "tell" to "yell" to "sell," to use Richard Moll's (1994) terms, with great interest, and I produced several long stories for that newspaper as well as one for the *Atlantic Monthly.* The topic made for good reading. UNK was by no means alone in pushing the envelope of good taste, and there was an abundance of man-bites-dog quotes from "enrollment managers" about how sleepy old Academe was finally getting with it and running itself like the "business that it really is." The word from Old Main was that undergraduate education was a product, and, like other products produced by large and expensive enterprises, it must be marketed. Administrators tended to make such statements with the zeal of the convert, as well as with a bit of arrogance.

The decision to plunge into the marketing of higher education proved to be fateful in at least two ways that few persons were prescient enough to anticipate at the time. First, sophisticated marketing efforts by colleges created a need for products to help students make sense of the literature overflowing their mailboxes. My own guide, the *Fiske Guide to Colleges,* was one such product, first appearing in 1982 as the *New York Times Selective Guide to Colleges.* It consists of essays on approximately three hundred of the "best and most interesting" colleges in the country, and it falls into Hunter's category of "narrative, subjective" guides. Information is gathered primarily through open-ended questionnaires sent to administrators and distributed by school officials to selected students. It uses a system of stars (actually a star, a telephone, and a bullet point) to rate the institutions on academic quality, social life, and the quality of life. Since 1982 the number of guides has proliferated, and new types have appeared, including those with the ranking and rating systems.

Second, the decision by colleges and universities to plunge into marketing created a new rhetoric for college admissions that permanently altered the relationship between institutions of higher education and prospective students. Applicants and their parents took institutions at their word that they were "customers." They started to do the things that consumers are supposed to do. They purchased the new guidebooks and other consumer aids, did sophisticated comparative shopping, and became bolder in making demands for counseling and other student services. The new seller-customer relationship was further complicated by the rising cost of getting a college education. Greater demand for student services increased institutional operating costs, which led to bigger tuition increases, which created the need for additional marketing strategies, and so forth. Today, students and their families have no qualms about using a generous financial aid offer from college A as a means of prying more aid out of college B. And why not? That is what one does if one is a sophisticated customer. And that is what the colleges told them they were.

Although college officials themselves took the first step down the slippery slope of redefining the college-applicant relationship, they were initially offended by the birth of the consumer movement in higher education. I recall participating in a particularly passionate panel discussion at a meeting of NACAC in Minneapolis shortly after the first edition of my own guide appeared. I was verbally chopped into little pieces and served for lunch by college admissions officers who told me, in no uncertain words, that I had no right as an outsider to make judgments about their institutions. Fortunately, attitudes have changed over the years. Admissions directors have come to sense the futility of viewing marketing as a one-way street. More important, they have decided that the guidebooks and rating systems are not going to go away and that a more prudent and fruitful approach is to attempt to influence the content. Some even see them as positive marketing opportunities. Thus, educational institutions and the guide publishers are now partners in an enterprise that over the years has taken on a life of its own. The relationship is complex, and it is important to understand how the roles and objectives of the two sides differ.

Purpose of Guidebooks. Bruce Hunter complains that "most of the guidebooks on the market do not make clear to the reading public what they are trying to do." Speaking only for my own guide, I beg to differ. *The Fiske Guide* is essentially a journalistic, or reporting, effort that replicates a process familiar to any college-bound student and his or her family. If a student is wondering whether to consider a particular college, it is natural to seek out current students or alumni and ask them about the place. The relevant questions in such situations do not tend to be the "big" questions about academic reputation or selectivity of admissions; these are givens. More to the point are topics such as the kinds of students that the college attracts, the intensity of the academic pressure, and whether students can have a good social life without joining a fraternity or sorority. Our student questionnaires duplicate this process of inquiry, except that we do it on a more systematic basis and cover far more colleges than any individual or family could do alone.

In addition to providing information about particular institutions, *The Fiske Guide* has another purpose: to broaden horizons. Perhaps the biggest strength of American higher education is its diversity. There are more than two thousand four-year colleges and universities in this country, and there are scores of institutions that would be a good match for any particular student. The problem is knowing that they exist. Too often a student's field of choice is limited by family traditions, peer pressure, fads, unimaginative guidance counseling, and other restrictive forces. *The Fiske Guide* offers students, parents, and counselors a means of taking off the blinders. No one is going to make a decision on where to attend college on the basis of a college guide write-up alone. But guides can, and often do, call students' attention to institutions that might not otherwise appear on their radar screens. College guides lend themselves to browsing, and to encourage this process we list each college's admissions "overlaps." If a student is interested in college A, there is a good chance that he or she might be interested in its major competitors. We suggest that students identify schools that they know they like, then read about these schools' overlaps, and then the overlaps of the overlaps and so forth.

Ratings and Risks. I also take issue with Hunter's statement that books "that assign arbitrary numbers to academic and quality-of-life ratings mislead students and distract them from the tasks of critical reading and careful research that should be at the heart of a good college search." *The Fiske Guide* uses a 1-to-5 system for the rating of academics, social life, and the quality of life. The ratings are by definition general and subjective, and the Introduction points out that "no complex institution can be described in terms of a single number or other symbol." At the same time, the ratings are a helpful tool in using the book. The core of the guide is the essays on each college, and the ratings represent a summary of the write-ups. There is nothing gnostic about the ratings; the reason for each of the ratings should be transparent from the text of the write-ups. Having decided on the kind of configuration that suits his or her needs, a student can then thumb through the book looking for other institutions with a similar set of ratings. The ratings do not mislead and distract. To the contrary, the whole point of *The Fiske Guide* is to facilitate a thoughtful search process. We believe it does just this.

Beyond my being eaten alive at professional conventions, there were certain risks inherent to producing the first edition of *The Fiske Guide*. The first was methodological and had to do with the fact that we left it up to admissions directors or other administrators to choose the students who would fill out the questionnaires. Could we trust such students to be honest? The answer, we discovered, was yes, at least when the answers were mailed directly back to us. American college students will tell it like it is. They tend to care about their institutions, but not in an uncritical way. They seem to understand that they would be doing no one a favor if readers were lured into making inappropriate choices.

The second risk was editorial. After writing about the umpteenth small liberal arts college in Ohio where "faculty members frequently invite students into their homes for dinner," would the colleges all sound alike? Once again we found no need to worry. Colleges and universities have distinct institutional characters and personalities, and these are not difficult to discern if one asks the right questions. Moreover, these characters and personalities remain relatively constant over long periods of time, a lesson I learned when doing the original write-up for my own alma mater, Wesleyan University. In the years following my graduation in 1959, Wesleyan more than doubled in size, went coed, and endured considerable disruption in the 1960s. Surely I, having graduated in prehistoric times, was the last person in the world in a position to say anything objective about Wesleyan. So I had three staff persons do drafts of the Wesleyan write-up before I sat down to do the final editing. It was an experience in déjà vu. What I discovered was that students in the 1980s were picking Wesleyan, rather than Yale or Amherst or other small liberal arts colleges, for the same reasons that my contemporaries and I did in the 1950s, reasons that had to do with the role of the individual in a social context. Despite the many changes that had transpired over two decades, the fundamental character and appeal of Wesleyan had remained constant.

Responses to Previous Chapters. For the reasons outlined above, I approached the other chapters in this volume with a conviction that it is possible, useful, and appropriate to report on colleges and universities in order to supply potential students with information that will help inform their choices of colleges or universities to attend. I read them with a mixture of admiration and disappointment. I admired the detailed and thoughtful analyses by several writers of the criteria that underlie various rankings of colleges and universities. I was glad to see Michael D. McGuire's critique of the validity of reputational studies, and I agree with much of what he says regarding the dangers of polluted data, frequent changes in the formulas, the arbitrariness of criteria, and the lack of adequate warnings to readers. Similarly, Bruce I. Mallette makes some well-founded observations, including the fact that figures on the percentages of students receiving financial aid often fail to distinguish among the sources of that aid. I also agree that the ratings tend to be biased toward institutional wealth and that little thought has gone into the question of what constitutes educational quality. On the latter point, however, I hasten to add that American colleges and universities themselves have given precious little thought to defining educational excellence.

I was disappointed, however, to discover—or at least to have my suspicions confirmed about—the paucity of research on how students and parents actually *use* guidebooks and rating systems. As Hossler and Foley state, "It is clear there is much we do not know about the impact of guidebooks, ratings, and many other sources of influence and information on the college enrollment decision." In the absence of solid research findings, few of the chapter authors are able to move beyond the obvious. It comes as no news to anyone that guidebooks and related products are used disproportionately by upper-middle-class families and that "low-income and first-generation college students are less likely to be influenced by or rely on guidebooks." Nor is it a revelation that nontraditional and commuting students, whose college-going options may be limited to the institutions down the street, "are not influenced by guide and ratings books."

Unfortunately, the absence of research did not preclude some authors from crawling out on some shaky limbs. Hossler and Foley observe, "Research to date suggests the impact of these sources is small." Maybe so, but it would have been nice to have a basis for making such a statement. They also suggest that maybe all the fuss is much ado about nothing, declaring, "There is some reason to question why guidebooks and ratings have received so much attention in recent years because of their limited impact on the decisions of students and parents." What are these reasons? If the impact is so limited, then why did we write chapters for this volume?

As the author of a college guide, I applaud pleas for more research on how the various products are actually used. I agree with Hossler and Foley that such research would also serve the interests of institutions. Perhaps publishers should start including warning labels, "The Secretary of Education has determined that lemminglike use of numerical ratings can be dangerous to your educational health."

I share the qualms of most contributors to this volume about rank ordering of colleges and universities. Accuracy and arbitrariness are problems, and there is really no way around the fact that numerical rankings constitute an effort to "quantify the unquantifiable." But my main problem with lists of "best colleges," especially those that put institutions in 1-2-3 order, relates to the implicit question that they purport to answer: What are the best colleges? The problem is that they do not go on to ask "for whom?" From the student's point of view, the relevant question is not "Which is the best college?" but "Which is the best college for me?"

Integrity of the Data. The various chapters in this volume tend to gloss over one topic that has received increased attention in the last year or so: the abuse of information by colleges and universities. The *Wall Street Journal* and other publications have carried stories documenting how institutions manipulate their reporting of SAT scores and other information in order to make themselves look better in the eyes of potential students. These stories, which contained confessions in direct quotes from officials of prestigious institutions, have been quite embarrassing to higher education, confirming in many people's minds the accusation that the admissions process is, as one writer put it, indeed something of a "charade." But they also cast doubt on the integrity of those of us on the receiving end of this information.

The problem of misleading information, however, is not new. Indeed, over the years we have made a number of changes in *The Fiske Guide* designed to minimize abuse of statistics. The most significant was a decision to stop publishing median SAT and ACT scores and to replace them with the ranges of the middle half of students—those from the twenty-fifth to the seventy-fifth percentiles. We did this for several reasons, starting with the fact that many students assumed that the single scores were cutoffs rather than medians. A student with a 460 verbal SAT score would look at an institution where the median was 480 and be intimidated, not realizing that his or her score was better than nearly half of the students at that institution. Another reason for the shift to ranges was to emphasize the statistical margin of error on SAT scores, which is more than 30 points either way. Finally, we wanted to deemphasize the importance of test scores. It is comforting and useful for students to know that their scores fall into the general ranges of a particular institution. If their scores are above the seventy-fifth percentile, they should ask themselves whether they would be better off in a more demanding environment. If their scores are below the twenty-fifth percentile, they might ask whether they will be pushing themselves. Beyond these relatively general questions, though, students and families should then stop thinking about SAT scores and make their choices on other criteria.

Standardized Data. I share the desire of various writers for more standardized data. I have become increasingly sensitive over the years to the burdens that we place on offices of institutional research, and I would certainly be glad to try to accommodate my own data needs to more uniform reporting. It would also be useful to get common agreement on the definition not only of SAT scores but of other pieces of data, such as student-faculty ratios. I also share the ambition for outcomes measurements but recognize the difficulties inherent to developing such measures and leave it to wiser heads to figure out what these should be. When they do, I shall be standing there with pen in hand.

Much has changed since UNK's aborted balloon launching. The nature of the relationship between applicants and institutions has been forever altered by the realities and the rhetoric of the marketplace. There is no turning back, no "innocence regained" to serve as sequel to "innocence lost." Institutions of higher education and publishers of guidebooks and other consumer products have very different goals, but they are also partners in an enterprise in which they both have an enormous stake. The challenge is to find ways of working together and serving their common clients: American students and their families.

KIMBERLY J. HOERITZ holds a M.S. Ed. in higher education administration from the University of Pennsylvania and is director of higher education research at Peterson's Guides, Princeton, New Jersey.

ALLAN B. CORDERMAN is chief executive officer and publisher at Wintergreen/Orchard House, Inc., in New Orleans, Louisiana, a major data provider to other publishers and a publisher of books, maps, software, and interest inventories for the professional college admissions and career planning markets.

MAX REED is senior editor of Barron's Profiles of American Colleges, *published by Barron's Educational Series, Inc., Hauppauge, New York.*

EDWARD B. FISKE is author of The Fiske Guide to Colleges *and* Smart Schools, Smart Kids *and is the former editor for the* New York Times.

*College rankings prepared by popular magazines have generated
considerable controversy in the higher education community.
Robert J. Morse of* U.S. News & World Report *and Jersey Gilbert,
formerly with* Money Magazine, *respond to the critics.*

Publishers' Perspectives: Magazines

Robert J. Morse, Jersey Gilbert

U.S. News & World Report's Philosophy Behind "America's Best Colleges" (Morse)

The purpose of the *U.S. News* response here is to comment on some of the major issues raised by the annual "America's Best Colleges" rankings. The other authors in this volume have thoughtfully analyzed the phenomenon of rankings, the statistical variables and the weights that *U.S. News* uses, and the weaknesses, problems, and sometimes even the strengths of the "America's Best Colleges" rankings. These factual and very detailed studies are possible because of the openness of *U.S. News* in providing virtually complete details on the ranking process.

Yet, these same authors sometimes forget that the main purpose of the *U.S. News* rankings is not to publish for a mass readership a document with a long, detailed statistical methodology spelled out over many pages. Surely, this type of presentation would be vital if the only readers of "America's Best Colleges" were members of the academic community. However, the main users of "America's Best Colleges" are prospective students and their parents. An academic document would be of limited interest to the overwhelming majority of our readers and would be a financial flop from a publishing point of view.

While "America's Best Colleges" is not as academically friendly as many would prefer, the higher education community has had a very significant impact on its continuing evolution. *U.S. News* is fully aware that its rankings and methodologies are read and analyzed with keen interest by many different individuals at institutions, including the presidents, the boards of trustees, the directors of admissions and public relations, alumni, current students, faculty, as well as institutional researchers. *U.S. News* also understands very clearly how those in higher education feel about the "America's Best Colleges" rankings as a result of feedback and comments. We meet with literally hundreds of senior college officials (an average of 2.5 per week) in our Washington, D.C., offices, and we attend many higher education conferences yearly. *U.S. News* has listened to the higher education community and the changes and improvements in its rankings process are proof of the *U.S. News* commitment to take the views of the higher education community seriously. This chapter provides another opportunity for *U.S. News* to give its side of the rankings debate.

Why Do Objective Third-Party Rankings Need to Be Done?   At a time when four years at a top-ranked private institution can cost more than the median home price, a prospective student and his or her parents need all the information possible about the comparative merits of colleges under consideration. There is little, if any, easily usable or obtainable comparative information of the relative merits of schools currently available to students and their parents. *U.S. News* feels that it is filling this void in higher education consumer information.

Students and their parents need to go beyond the information that colleges provide either through viewbooks or other school-published brochures. School-provided data are generally limited in scope, not published in a comparative way to a school's peer institutions, and sometimes are very self-serving and misleading. They are generally published in a way that makes the school appear in the best possible light.

Parents and students need and are demanding, based on the response that "America's Best Colleges" has achieved in the marketplace, a third party that can make an objective analysis, with easy-to-use statistical comparisons and carefully collected up-to-date information on the relative merits of various kinds of institutions in different educational categories. It is very clear, based on the cost and complexity of data gathering from colleges, that an individual student or parent would be unable to collect the information that *U.S. News* obtains and publishes yearly. Students and parents either would be denied the data or they would be intimidated by the process of trying to get the information.

Consumers, who in this case are prospective students and their parents, are used to getting comprehensive, current, and comparative information on major purchases, such as a new car or a health care plan, which generally are less expensive than four to six years at college. *U.S. News* strongly believes that comparative information that measures the relative merits of institutions should be available when students consider a college education that, in some cases, now costs nearly $120,000.

Why Is Reputation So Important?   One of the major complaints in the academic community against the *U.S. News* rankings is that there is too great a weight put on academic reputation (currently 25 percent). Critics contend that the academics who are the respondents to our survey have little knowledge about other schools, or that reputations are either based on faculty who have retired, or that schools that are up-and-coming academically are unable to move up in such a poll because of the lag in creating and losing a reputation.

U.S. News believes that, fairly or unfairly, the name of a top-ranked college or university on a résumé opens more doors to jobs and graduate schools than does the name of a school in the bottom tier. This is especially true for the early years in the workplace. In today's tight job market for new college graduates, any leg up on their competitors can be important.

U.S. News recognizes that while few of the nearly three thousand top college officials who yearly respond to the survey can be familiar with every school in a given category, collectively they know far more than is known by any individual reader. Prospective students, parents, graduate school admissions officers, large donors, alumni, foundations, college guidance counselors, as well as those making hiring decisions are looking at reputational ranking as one of many criteria in choosing a college, admitting a student, giving money, making a grant, or hiring a new employer. The bottom line in today's world is that reputation does matter to a variety of constituencies.

How We Work with the Higher Education Community to Improve Our Rankings. U.S. News prides itself on the access it has been able to achieve with experts and officials in the higher education community. U.S. News will continue to have an open-door policy in regard to meeting virtually anytime during the year with those in higher education, either at our Washington, D.C., editorial offices or at educational forums such as the annual Association for Institutional Research (AIR) conferences. Members of the "America's Best Colleges" staff are willing to appear before almost any educational groups to discuss the rankings or higher education in general.

This ongoing dialogue with college officials is the forum where U.S. News receives, as well as solicits, ideas and criticism about refining its methodology. By constantly listening to our critics and asking questions about the variables that can and should be measured, the education of the U.S. News staff is enhanced. If suggestions prove both relevant and practical, we adopt them in future surveys or calculations. U.S. News screens ideas carefully and knows that in some cases methodological changes are made for purely self-serving reasons. Many of the suggestions that result in improvements in the methodology have come from the institutional research community.

U.S. News will continue to be open about its rankings process, the methodology, the weights, the surveys that are used, and the results. If there is going to be an open exchange of views about "America's Best Colleges," which there is currently, it is important that it be based on what U.S. News is actually doing.

Why We Change the System. One of the issues among higher education researchers is that changing the methodology from one year to the next causes volatility in the rankings, when institutions themselves change very little from year to year. They argue that this methodologically induced volatility makes it hard, if not impossible, to make time line comparisons.

There is a great deal of irony in this argument. Higher education cannot have it both ways. Improvement means change. In order for U.S. News to act on suggestions as well as improve on weaknesses in its system, the methodology must necessarily change. If *U.S. News* followed the opposite course, we would be accused of maintaining the status quo. These changes, which of course add volatility to the rankings, come from ideas generated by the education community. So the question becomes, Is it better to stay with a measure that is flawed or could obviously be improved just so the rankings will not change? Also, if new systems are developed to measure outcomes or assessments of what graduates learn at college, should *U.S. News* ignore them? *U.S. News* feels that the answers to both of these questions is no!

Changes in methodology result in an improved product for the consumer. Sticking with a ranking that can be improved is not what *U.S. News* readers expect. They expect *U.S. News* to come up with the best ways each year to rank schools, even if it means changing the system from one year to the next. If a significantly better way exists to define a question, collect information, do a calculation, or measure an aspect of what is going on in higher education, it is the *U.S. News* policy to implement those changes.

Data Integrity. Clearly, the quality of the information that *U.S. News* uses in its rankings is the most important aspect of the annual survey. *U.S. News* believes strongly that it is incumbent on us to make certain that the data we provide our readers are as credible as possible, given the limitations imposed by self-reported information and our lack of power to audit any specific school's admissions office books.

U.S. News currently has a multistep data integrity system in place to ensure the veracity of the information we publish. As part of this process, starting in 1995, *U.S. News* now does all its own data collection in order to improve quality control. As a result of numerous checks, *U.S. News* believes that the overwhelming majority of colleges provide data for our survey that they feel are accurate. It is clear to me, having served as manager of the in-house *U.S. News* data collection process, that many of the fourteen hundred colleges in the *U.S. News* universe lack a consistent internal system for collecting accurate institutional information and for filing external surveys. In other words, many data problems are the result of lack of caring or sloppy reporting practices.

As for the others, *U.S. News* is surprised that some institutions, which enforce honor codes for their students and regularly teach the importance of personal values, would allow a few of their officials to knowingly submit false information for publication in a national magazine. In the end, data integrity begins with the leadership at each school setting the standard that only correct information will be submitted on external surveys, and putting a system in place that makes it happen.

U.S. News has taken a number of initiatives to ensure the integrity of the data for "America's Best Colleges." First, the statistical questionnaire that is at the heart of the annual survey was subjected to a rigorous review by a cross section of college and university admissions and financial aid officers at an annual meeting held at *U.S. News*. Then, before the questionnaire was printed and sent to schools, it was circulated among the same admissions and financial aid group. In addition, we circulated the surveys among the Higher Education Data Policy Committee of AIR for comment. The goal: maximum consistency and clarity of the questions we asked each school, as well as maximum rigor in defining the exact nature of the data sought.

Second, on the advice of the institutional research community, U.S. News has asked for information, whenever possible, that comes directly from external reports such as the Integrated Postsecondary Education Data System enrollment and finance surveys that schools file with the U.S. Department of Education. This approach allows for the use of standard definitions, which reduces the data collection burden as well as increases the comparative quality of the information.

Third, the U.S. News data base has been programmed to flag data that are internally inconsistent or that appear incorrect. These edit checks act as triggers, such as when an institution reports that it has more faculty who hold terminal degrees in their fields than the overall number of faculty on its teaching staff.

Fourth, on the premise that a specific school's data change very little from year to year, U.S. News has also programmed variance checks that compare how a school's data have changed from what were submitted previously. These variance checks, which also have been worked out with advice from the institutional research community, also flag a change in a school's Scholastic Aptitude Test and American College Test scores or retention rates, if those increases or decreases are greater than the average change for all schools for that specific data element.

Fifth, U.S. News is entering into a cooperative arrangement with one of the major bond rating services that will enable us to cross-check information we receive from many colleges with some of the same data that schools annually supply to these rating agencies. Similarly, U.S. News is arranging to cross-check graduation rates against data that Division I institutions are required to file yearly with the National Collegiate Athletic Association.

Sixth, with its 1995 survey, U.S. News initiated efforts to ensure a level statistical playing field. We asked each college whether the data they provided in the section on entrance scores and class standing included the scores of all entering students. If the response was no, we then telephoned the school to ask for information on the excluded students. If the school again refused to provide the data, we then estimated, in accord with acceptable statistical practices, the missing scores. This estimate was included among the data elements used to determine the school's ranking. Data that represent estimates are so indicated in the rankings tables.

Seventh, the names of the handful of institutions that refuse our many requests to provide data for the survey (including requests made in accord with various state freedom of information laws) will be prominently displayed in both the annual U.S. News guidebook and magazine issue devoted to "America's Best Colleges." And, although they choose not to respond, these schools will still be included in the ranking tables. The ranking will be determined by a combination of the scores achieved by these schools in the separate reputational survey and by appropriate estimates of the educational data they choose not to provide. These schools will be appropriately identified in the tables.

Finally, *U.S. News* continues its data verification procedure, which asks each school to recheck and verify the data that we publish. This is the only complete verification process done by any publisher.

Conclusion. The editors of *U.S. News* welcome suggestions for additional steps that we might take to further ensure the integrity of "America's Best Colleges." In the end, however, we must depend on the good faith and honesty of the institutions to whom society also entrusts its ideas, its ideals, and its young. When we began publishing this annual survey, we did so with the belief that ultimately we could rely on the good faith and honesty of America's colleges and universities. We still feel the same way.

Money Magazine (Gilbert)

It is impossible to invent a ranking or rating system that is free of blindspots. That may sound like a strange opening statement from someone who spent a good part of five years (1990 to 1994) developing system for rating the price and value trade-offs at America's colleges and universities. But just because one recognizes that such systems will inevitably have their limitations does not mean that working on such systems is wasted effort. While all rankings are flawed in one or more respects, it is also true that most of them—at least those that are not outright fabrications—are interesting or useful in some fashion. If there is any middle ground in the controversy over magazine rankings, it is this: The critics should concede that comparative studies have intrinsic merit and, at the least, can be used to launch discussions about college search or quality issues. On the other side, the media should resist the temptation to overstate the applicability of the findings.

U.S. News & World Report. In a world well stocked with comparative data, the initial 1983 *U.S. News* survey of college presidents (*U.S. News* only added deans and admissions officers to its survey in 1989) should not have caused much commotion. The question it posed is a perfectly legitimate if limited research question: Which colleges do college presidents think offer the best undergraduate education? If nothing else, the survey acts as a record of outlook changes among leaders of higher education. Surely, in a small way the survey findings contribute to the debate over comparative quality, even if we all agree that the opinions of college presidents are not as helpful to the consumer as, say, a survey of large employers or of admissions officers at graduate and professional schools. It seems strange to argue that college presidents' opinions are completely irrelevant.

Trouble is, some critics have been reduced to arguing just that. *U.S. News'* rankings appeared in an imperfect world. By compelling the results, ranking the colleges mentioned, and calling the article "America's Best Colleges," the editors seemed to ascribe much more significance to the findings than the findings merited. Unlike most critics, it is my contention that this transgression was not the main root of the problem. Let us say that *U.S. News* had been more honest and called its rankings "College Presidents Tell Us Which Schools They

Think Have America's Best Undergraduate Colleges" (a perfectly awful cover line even if more accurate). How long would it take before the general public began referring to the annual article in a more convenient shorthand, namely, "Best Colleges"?

The real difficulty here is that *U.S. News* has no competition in the "best" business. For better or for worse, it is *the list*—the only rating that attempts to regularly compare expert opinions about institutional quality (as well as some institutional measures of quality) in higher education. Should we really be surprised that *U.S. News'* marketing, publicity, and headline copywriters exploit that position? If AIR or any other higher education special interest group is serious about the claim that magazine rankings may be treated in an uncritical fashion by high school students and their parents, it needs to encourage more rankings and lists, not less.

Why more? Three decades' worth of criticism directed at available college performance measures has failed to capture the public's attention. That is unfortunate, because I do think the debate over how to measure success and failure in higher education programs is important. The failing is not lack of theoretical insight. Traditional views of what colleges do have been challenged from numerous angles. Blindspots have been identified and strong, plausible cases have been made for various alternative measures. Naturally, the alternative measures themselves have alternative blindspots, but that is true in any field. Blindspots should not be used as an excuse to stifle comparative analysis.

If one really wants to shift the public focus from the beauty pageant aspect of the *U.S. News* rankings to an appreciation of the factors behind them and how those factors bear on the results, these alternative insights into institutional measurement need to be made operational. Until someone does, it will be hard to imagine that the public will take critics' views seriously. The public is not interested in the sterile debate over epistemology and methodology. It wants the debate to lead to something that makes real-world choices easier. Readers need concrete help with specific problems.

In other words, name names. If someone thinks one way of looking at quality is biased against certain institutions or classes of institutions, just proving that the bias might exist is not sufficient. The challenge is to produce an alternative screen that helps readers worried about that bias to redirect their attention to alternative institutions. The public will begin to compare both lists and understand the strengths and weaknesses of each list better. That will give consumers something concrete to evaluate and that is all they need.

How Smart Is the Reader? There is a tendency among critics of magazine and college guide compilations to treat consumers as if they are clueless, belittling their appetite for lists and treating it as a kind of social failure. That view is unfair. Readers of magazines such as *Money* are analytically sophisticated, or at least trying to be.

When confronted with different ranked lists, they are quite capable of recognizing the connection between a specific set of sorting criteria and the resulting ordered outcome. After all, that is essentially what an investment screen is:

the systematic application of selected criteria to a problem of ordering choice. Financial journalists and their readers live comfortably in a world where even highly respected ranking schemes are known by their blindspots as well as their strengths.

For instance, if I want to talk about trends among the biggest companies, I might turn to the Fortune 500 for a list of the largest U.S. publicly owned corporations ranked by sales. Of course, behemoth privately owned companies like Bechtel and United Parcel Service will not be there. Major U.S. corporations like Columbia Pictures and First Boston that are owned by foreign companies will not be there. Companies that are large by virtue of market capitalization, assets, profits, or employees but not sales will not be there. On the other hand, choosing a list of the largest companies based on any of those other criteria—say, market cap as represented by the Standard and Poor's 500—would omit another, different set of companies. The fact that a "definitive" list of the nation's largest companies cannot be compiled does not paralyze financial analysis. The full menu of rankings only serves to help.

Note that I am not advocating ignoring the ranking's blindspots. Good practice requires that one consider how the choice of one list or the other might affect conclusions drawn from one ranking or the other. And, in fact, editorial lineups in the best investing magazines often offer items devoted to the pros and cons of different investment and financial indexes or the pros and cons of different ways of measuring mutual fund performance (see, for example, Morrow, 1994).

Unfortunately, when readers go from investing choices to college choices, they are given very little scope within which to exercise their analytical sophistication. Debra L. Stuart (this volume) is quite right to speak of a "hunger for digested information." The thing we have to remember is that the hunger comes as much from an increasing ability to assess and utilize complex digested data in other aspects of our culture. That aspect of the appetite is not served by restricting the information diet; far better to assume the alimentary tract is sound and expand the menu.

Finding Better Ways to Serve the Reader: *Money Guide: Your Best College Buys Now.* To a large extent, expanding the menu was what *Money* had in mind when it embarked on its price-value study in 1990. Families engaged in the college search process were almost entirely left to their own devices when trying to decide if the cost of education at one institution was warranted by that school's program. This state of affairs existed in spite of the increasingly heavy financial burdens placed on students and parents. The higher education community greeted *Money* with almost as much hostility as it had welcomed *U.S. News*. Although this time around the offending study was on firmer, if not completely solid, methodological ground, it seemed to make little difference to critics. Actually, the editors were not that surprised. As a general rule, anyone who publishes an ordered listing or systematic rating system can expect to immediately generate a whole new cottage industry devoted solely to the identification and description of the blindspots in the publisher's methodology. Before I discuss the blindspots and what can and cannot be done about them, it is important to describe some of the strengths of *Money*'s approach.

Foremost, *Money* was up-front in defining the applicability of its rankings—at least until recently. The very first issue contained the following cautionary note: "While our rankings highlight those colleges providing strong educations at prices that are more than fair, they are by no means intended to be a definitive guide to college choice. When shopping for a school, you will want to consider numerous other criteria" (*Money Guide . . .* , 1990, p. 72). A similar piece of advice was printed in each subsequent year until dropped in the 1995 edition.

We can admit up front that the tuition-value-benefit analysis that would most benefit each prospective college student would be one that customized the analysis to account for that student's own unique matrix of probabilities: for example, the probabilities that the student will end up choosing one major over another, that the student will want to go to graduate school or professional school versus will start working after graduating, that the student will qualify for or negotiate a scholarship, that the particular set of schools selected will offer the student an in-state discount, that the financial resources available to the student and the student's family will be sufficient, and so on. No published source can do that. No researcher can do that.

Published analysis can serve the consumer, however, if it targets benchmark features of compared products. By benchmark feature I mean a prominent and stable aspect of the product or service against which the consumer can gauge his or her own circumstances. The most important benchmark of any major product is the listed price. Consumers will make their final judgments about value based on any discounted price, but in order to do that they have to be able to put the sticker price itself in a meaningful framework. Thus, *Consumer Reports* rates products on the basis of sticker price, even though the editors and the readers are fully aware that for big-ticket items like cars and appliances, most individuals actually pay a reduced or sale price.

Significance of Official Tuition. In the rush to point out how many students end up paying reduced tuitions, many critics of *Money* have overlooked the market impact of official tuition schedules. (*Money,* in effect, defines official price as the full undergraduate tuition charged at private schools or the full out-of-state student tuition charged at public schools.) When college officials set the tuition schedule, whether they like it or not they make a declaration that their undergraduate education is worth at least that much. And note that with a few exceptions, they make the claim equally for all the undergraduate departments institutionwide, good and bad.

Granted, when members of the board of trustees (or whatever oversight authority is responsible) get together to vote on tuition increases, they may not discuss pricing in those terms. The public, however, perceives it so. (The only other consumer conclusion would be that the institution is a relatively inefficient producer of educational services and is deliberately overcharging at least some part of its clientele.) Therefore, the official tuition, whether actually paid by any given student, remains a compelling comparative benchmark for all undergraduates. On that basis alone, *Money's* rankings, presented without fanfare, deserve a read.

Analyzing tuitions makes for an especially compelling comparative investigation at a time when there is so much confusion and debate about concepts of comparative educational value. We still encounter officials who defend tuition increases or their own institution's high tuition level on the grounds that the difference between what a graduate will earn over his or her lifetime and what a nongraduate will earn more than makes up for the four-year cost. This defense confuses two economic issues. If I buy a $2,000 computer to write a book, the value of that computer is not the $25,000 advance that I would not have earned if I tried to type the book on my old Royal manual. The value of the computer is the opportunity cost of $1,500 that I should have paid for a better-priced comparable computer of another make. A college is overvalued if a student can get the same education at another institution for less expenditure, underpriced if the student would have to pay more elsewhere.

Granted, my view of comparisons based on official prices has its critics. They say it is unfair to compare all schools as if they produce the same product. The argument that colleges have different missions has merit, but it has been overdone in the criticism. Yes, there are a number of institutions of higher education that truly provide a different educational product. Two-year colleges, religious colleges, and some subject-limited specialty schools come to mind. But most four-year colleges and universities are offering the same service: a series of related majors leading to a unified credential that opens roughly the same range of career doors. The methods educators employ to produce the result may differ, and the clients they attract may be cut from different parts of the demographic fabric, but the final manifestation, the degree, is the same commodity. At least, that is the cultural mystique.

In fact, most four-year college mission statements fail to draw sharp distinctions among institutional goals. The platitudes are interchangeable. Most colleges claim a broad range of educational goals; they try to be all things to all students. One has only to sit down and read a hundred or so mission statements within forty-eight hours to know why future anthropologists can be forgiven for thinking that all college mission statements are descended from the same nineteenth-century mission statement named Lucy.

It is also worth noting in this connection that after a thorough review of the literature on college impact, Pascarella and Terenzini (1991, p. 597) came to the following conclusion: "Beyond [a] few small impacts, however, institutional categorizations such as the Carnegie classification appear to tell us little about differences in between-college impacts. Perhaps even more than indexes of college quality, classifications such as research university, comprehensive private university, and liberal arts college may, as suggested, simply conceal so much between-college variability within each classification that consistent impacts on students cannot be found."

Some Students Actually Pay the Official Price. The defense of *Money*'s choice of official tuition as the dependent variable in its model goes beyond the symbolic benchmark value of price. Students who eventually enter college paying full official prices will find the price choice entirely appropriate and practical. How large an undergraduate group is that? It is hard to say with certainty, but one can establish a reliable minimum yearly figure by consulting the financial aid questions asked in either the Wintergreen/Orchard House or Peterson's annual college survey.

For example, of the 664,000 first-year students attending the 838 colleges in the *Money* study base that provided information to Peterson's for 1991, just over 317,000 students received no financial aid of any kind. (The propensity to grant financial aid appeared largely independent of college price. For instance, the 50 most expensive institutions distributed aid to 46 percent of their first-year students. The average for all institutions was 52 percent.) About one-third attended private colleges, so they paid full tuition. Of the remaining 200,000 or so at public schools, we need to make an estimate, since the data are not broken down by in-state and out-of-state students. If we assume that the 20 percent average out-of-state population at public schools held for both the aided and unaided group, that suggests about 40,000 out-of-state students without financial aid. (The assumption is simply that out-of-state students are not more or less aided than residents, which is a conservative assumption.)

So the minimum total number of first-year students paying what *Money* defines as official tuition is 140,000 per year. The number is probably considerably higher for the following reasons: (1) The 838 institutions reporting information on financial aid were only a partial accounting of the schools in the *Money* study that year. (2) Many schools include students aided with loans in their count of students receiving financial aid; however, for pricing purposes, a loan is not a reduction in tuition any more than a mortgage (including a subsidized mortgage) reduces the price of a house to the downpayment amount. (3) Some schools report outside scholarships as a form of financial aid. It certainly is financial aid, but if the outside scholarship is unrestricted in nature (that is, can be applied to tuition at any school), it does not constitute a reduction of that particular school's price. For this estimate, such aid would not apply to the calculation.

What should be clear from these estimates is that *Money*'s price target is the relevant tuition choice matrix for a sizable readership drawn from the demographic group that the magazine was created to serve. Furthermore, one can easily envision a way of making the price matrix more serviceable for an even wider audience. With the potential of on-line, interactive versions of national magazines, *Money*'s publishers could provide any one of fifty "customized" rankings available to readers who indicate their state residency. A program could substitute a limited selection of appropriate resident tuition rate for each state-specific, public, nonresident tuition compiled in the basic model. That pricing feature would amount to a virtual reality price menu for about half the students. Making such a program available would also go a long way toward clarifying the applicability of the basic hard-copy ranking published in the annual edition.

Sensitivities of the Money Model. Beyond the price applicability issue, how much insight consumers derive from the price-value study depends in large part on the selection and measurement of the independent variables. I cannot deny that there are also legitimate issues concerning the choice of statistical tools and other elements of model design. Different model designs may lead to conflicting results when applied to the same data. In the case of the *Money* regression model, however, this does not seem to be as significant a concern in regard to the final list of best buys.

In order to test the sensitivity of the *Money* rankings to the use of regression techniques, a "neutral" model design was applied to the 1992 data and again to the 1993 data. The neutral model simply gave equal weights to the sixteen independent variables used in the actual ranking model. Each school's sixteen scores were standardized and then summed with equal weight. Finally, the standardized score of the sum was compared with the z-score of that school's tuition. Colleges with aggregate summed, independent variable scores below the mean were dropped and then the list was ranked by greatest positive discrepancy of summed scores over tuition scores. (This parallels the procedure in the actual *Money* ranking whereby the institutions with predicted tuition-quality values below average are screened out before the final best buy lists are chosen.) Both years the neutral model would have chosen nine of the top ten value-ranked schools for that year. The neutral model also chose between eighty and ninety of the top one hundred *Money* college buys each year. The point here is that anyone critical of the actual names on the best buys list published by *Money* should understand that the choice of the quality factors in the independent variable matrix is probably the most influential element in determining that list.

Given the findings of the neutral model test, most of *Money*'s research in 1993 and 1994 was focused on issues that surround the selection of independent variables and the factors that affect their measurement. The measurement problem, in fact, was already well appreciated since the first edition. At that time, the naive mistake of accepting institutionally supplied data at face value led to misleading results. Consequently, the editors initiated regular data verification sequences triggered by year-to-year or agency-to-agency discrepancies in data reported from the same institution. Furthermore, they designed their own questionnaire in an attempt to gain greater control over the quality of key information.

As a result of the verification effort, *Money*, along with *U.S. News*, now has some of the cleanest data sets publicly available for the statistics that they collect. This effort still has a long way to go, but eventually the media, the bond rating agencies, state governments, and the federal government will force higher education to get its disclosure standards in order. Unfortunately, until then, the extensive process of data verification restrains magazine-initiated research on the operational problems of defining, measuring, and comparing quality.

Independent Variables and Issues of Quality. For *Money* in particular, with only sixteen operational variables representing educational quality, the price-value model is open to the charge that it presents a rather restricted account of college effectiveness. Clearly there are gaps.

Some gaps are not likely to be filled. I doubt we will ever see a variable for campus beauty, even though an attractive setting is something consumers undoubtedly pay more for. The difficulty is coming up with a measurement that everyone can agree on.

Fortunately, omission of factors, such as campus beauty, that depend on individual tastes is not a matter of great concern. Consumers routinely adapt information about benchmark measures to better reflect their subjective predilections for other, nonbenchmark factors.

The gaps that should concern users are the missing measures of educational resources and educational effectiveness that by their nature are not readily apparent to the consumer: for instance, data on the amount of individual attention given each student, the amount of computer resources and support available, the degree of faculty dedication to teaching, the success of the skills support programs in writing and math, and the fitness of the labs and other teaching aids. The list of resource factors can easily be extended. Likewise, extremely important outcomes measures are missing. How quickly do graduates get jobs? Once they get in, how well do they perform in graduate and professional schools? How satisfied with their education will they be ten years from now?

In particular, the whole facet of teaching efficacy is not well addressed in either of the magazine ranking schemes. At best, different types of student-faculty ratios serve as proxies for faculty availability. *Money* pushes the usual proxy ratios one step further by trying to limit the faculty denominator to "faculty members who actually taught in a given period." In addition, after a methodologically unsatisfying adjustment for institutions with graduate schools, *Money* reported expenditures on instruction. Unfortunately, neither of these proxies effectively targets the more important questions: How good is the teaching? How effectively is the instructional budget spent?

On the other hand, that the magazine rankings models do not effectively address the question of instructional quality should come as no shock to anyone involved in higher education. Controversy over how to measure the impact of teaching and the relative merits of different instructional approaches has been a central feature on the campus landscape for the past thirty years.

In fact, what can be said about the uncertainty over evaluation of college instruction applies in general to the whole issue of measuring college quality. Look around at the fragmented vision of quality projected by institutions of higher education. While the more activist members of the instructional research community try to impress the educational leadership with new perspectives on pedagogy, admissions directors all over the country boast of their efforts to attract students with higher entrance examination scores, faculty chairs trumpet their colleagues' newest publications and preen when they hire professors with impressive publications, and college presidents proudly show off new buildings. The press releases cite all these things as evidence of institutional improvement. Magazines get bombarded with much more of that kind of "evidence" than anything else. If institutional researchers are critical of the pace at which the magazines and guidebooks adopt measurements reflecting the latest data on institutional effectiveness, they have to understand that the media are concurrently pulled in many directions.

Many editors are sympathetic to measures of institutional effectiveness that promise to be more consumer friendly. Once again, unfortunately, there is a gap between the advocacy of new measures and the availability of the data on which to base comparative analysis. Editors and guidebook publishers would like to break free of reliance on traditional indicators such as student-faculty ratio and move toward providing comparative information about the quality of the interactions between faculty and students. Which schools really create a teaching culture centered on student needs? And how do we know this?

As long as there are no widely accepted indicators of teaching effectiveness, the default indicator is reputation for teaching effectiveness. The same observation can be made about career outcomes measures. As long as they are rather limited in availability, the default indicator becomes the alumni's reputations for success. *Money* deliberately avoided using reputational indicators in its model due to a healthy skepticism about their reliability. Not everyone will be so circumspect, least of all the marketing departments of the colleges themselves. As long as there is a vacuum of rigorous indicators for crucial aspects of institutional effectiveness, college publicists are free to fill the void with claims of having a good reputation for this or that. Meanwhile, the downside for *Money* is that its model appears limited.

As long as the magazine is up-front about the limitations that currently beset the search for indicators of comparative quality, a limited model is better than no model at all. After all, the purpose of the study is to identify schools that are underpriced in some respect. The best buys, in fact, are underpriced on the basis of the indicators studied.

Sooner or later curiosity would have led someone to a similar set of research initiatives. The readily available body of college quality measures—flawed, limitations, and all—has long been bandied about by college officials, by college guidebooks, and by serious researchers seeking to screen for the effects of institutional characteristics on their findings. It seems only natural to ask if there are meaningful statistical relationships between such widely employed indicators and the tuition levels of colleges and universities.

The U.S. Department of Education published just such a study examining the correlations between various indicators and prices (Gilmore, 1991). *Money*'s methodology just goes one step further. It threw out the variables with low correlations to price and aggregated the remaining indicators in a ranking model. Oh yes, and the magazine named names.

If there is a logical justification for *Money*'s price-value study, and if the editors underscore that these measures may not be of significance to everyone or that these measures do not tell the whole story, the magazine seems well within the bounds of its mandate. A reader sees the list of indicators and can judge if they are meaningful benchmarks for his or her purposes. On the other hand, dropping the cautionary note referred to above from the 1995 edition and hyping other claims, as chronicled by Mallette (this volume), reflect a disturbing trend. We can only hope the editors rectify this in future editions.

Priced Quality. There is another dimension to *Money*'s choice of independent variables that is not always fully appreciated by critics. Initially, the editors were not interested in incorporating all possible conceptions of educational quality in their model. Since the point was, and is, to find value in the marketplace, they chose to focus on a subset of quality that we can call "priced quality." In this empirically based view, the greatest weight is given to educational features and outcomes that are most strongly associated with higher prices. The operative definition of value then is "getting features that are usually priced higher for less." Philosophically, what the market values may not be good, but the idea of priced quality avoids making those judgments.

Looked at this way, it is easier to understand some of the choices made in building the model, especially in the area of resource variables. For instance, the point has been made that the extensive use of interlibrary loans has, in effect, expanded the collections of all campus libraries, if one roughly knows the title needed and is willing to wait for it to be delivered. All that is true, but since this service, in one form or another, is widespread, there should not be a price premium placed on it. The premium comes from having a large library collection conveniently at hand. The strength of the library size-price correlation is monitored by *Money*'s researchers every year. Should that begin to fall off, the library variable may become obsolete. Until electric sharing technology includes immediate on-line text transmission, however, I suspect that *Money* will continue to make the shared library adjustment only for those situations like the Claremont Colleges, where the shared facilities are in close proximity to one another.

Money monitors the correlations between various indicators and tuition each year. Many of the monitored relationships involve variables that are not currently part of the ranking model. In the meantime, only the ones currently showing the strongest "priced" behavior are included in the model. That choice may change if the market shifts the directions of its pricing premiums, that is, if college administrators, students, and parents come to value other qualities in higher education. The institutional research community has very strong opinions about what constitutes effectiveness in education. That is as it should be; but if the outlook is not shared by the consuming public or by the college administrators who set the prices of undergraduate degrees, those ideas are left in a kind of limbo for the sake of constructing a pricing model. For example, *Money* had done some preliminary work on the possibility of adding a variable based on the concept of value added or net effect. Even if the editors had never read the work of researchers like Astin (1992), they would have been drawn to this possibility from a simple examination of the cross-correlation coefficients among various variables in the model.

The sixteen variables in the price-value model are grouped into four regression variables to take advantage of the strong correlations among related variables. The grouped variables tend to have correlation coefficients above .73. The selectivity variables in particular have values above .80. By the same token, however, they had fair to middling cross-correlation coefficient values with the short- and long-term outcomes variables, namely, retention, graduation rates, and Ph.D. frequencies. These values ranged from .52 to .65. None of this should surprise anyone familiar with the strong effects that precollege characteristics have on outcomes.

To test the viability of including a value-added-type variable, *Money* regressed various outcomes measures against selectivity, such as entrance examination scores and high school class rank. Although all the possible combinations involving all the available data were not computed, it became clear very quickly that the resulting residual measures—the proxy value-added variables—had very weak relationships with tuition pricing when they were correlated with tuitions. The coefficient values were all below .35, averaging around .28. As of 1994, all the other variables included in the *Money* model correlate at .38 to .68 with tuition. One can interpret these findings as evidence that the market does not place much value on the ability of colleges to achieve outcomes in excess of what we would expect given their selectivity patterns.

This attitude may change in time. And the findings were at least positive and significant that there is some small relationship. In the meantime, *Money* does not yet include a value-added variable in its model. To some extent the model already has a bias in that direction. The high cross-correlations between the selectivity measures and the outcomes measures work to reduce the value of the coefficient of the selectivity regression variable. One can see the bias when one compares the results of the neutral model, which gives greater weight to the selectivity variables, and the best buys model. The schools missing in the best buys list but present in the neutral model are mostly schools whose first-year students have relatively high entrance examination scores and high grade point averages, but whose outcomes statistics lag behind other schools with the same selectivity patterns.

Looking Ahead. We should not assume that either of the annual magazine rankings will ossify in their current form. As textbook writers are fond of pointing out, research, especially multivariate analysis, is an iterative process whereby current results lead constantly to new questions, further inquiry, and new modifications (see, for instance, Johnson and Wichern, 1992). The fact that both *Money* and *U.S. News* started out asking rather modest research questions and slowly introduced changes in their methodologies should not be held against them. Research starts with the familiar and moves on from there. All that we should really require is a commitment to follow through on the process. To some extent, that commitment has already been demonstrated by the amount of time and effort devoted to cleaning up the data series employed in their models.

What worries me about recent proposals advanced by Anne Machung (this volume) and others is that the iterative process will be hobbled. The initiative for gathering comparative information has always come from the guide-books, the media, and state and federal governments. Until the colleges themselves mount credible efforts to provide comparative institutional evaluations, the need for comparative data will, by default, be defined by outside agencies. Critics cannot, on the one hand, complain about "unenlightened" methodology and then, on the other hand, cut off access to data requests designed to test new approaches and iterative evolution of that methodology.

It is true that the information disclosure burden placed on institutional research is growing. That, however, is a reflection of the increasing social, intellectual, and now economic stature accorded the data that have come into the care of institutional researchers. No one objects to trying to organize the data request process so as to reduce the burden. At the same time, we have to ensure that the media are not prevented from extending and enriching their ability to analyze comparative data in ways that better serve the public.

ROBERT J. MORSE *is senior editor and director of data analysis of* U.S. News & World Report's *"America's Best Colleges."*

JERSEY GILBERT *is senior reporter for* Smart Money *and former editor of* Money Guide: Your Best College Buys Now *for* Money Magazine.

This chapter provides a framework and questions for developing
a research design to improve college guides and ratings.

A Research Agenda

Josetta S. McLaughlin, Gerald W. McLaughlin

Drawing on the previous chapters, we conclude the volume by identifying needed research. When considering appropriate research, many of us think of the traditional hypothesis-testing processes with classical random assignment and controls. To examine college guides and rankings, however, research needs to be multifaceted (Simon, 1991). Guidebooks do not exist in a neat vacuum where research can be done with classical research designs, devoid of politics and profits. Successfully converting guides into positive vehicles that are fair to major stakeholders and customers alike requires that we consider both their content and the context within which they are used.

In this concluding chapter, we first recommend an operational framework for identifying research questions. The framework identifies a systematic way to ask a complete set of questions about how to improve the guides. Then we look at several major questions that must be answered about the context of improving the contribution of guidebooks and their ratings to various customers. This second part examines the environment in which the guidebooks are used. What kind of research will make guides and ratings a valued contribution financially and help ensure that they are fair to various stakeholders given the environment in which they are used?

Technical Issues

Views expressed in earlier chapters of this volume suggest that college guidebooks are permanent fixtures on the academic landscape. The message is unmistakably clear: There is a demand for a product that provides credible information on institutions of higher learning. We are challenged to use our unique skills to improve the ability of various customers to make decisions about the characteristics of our colleges. The ability of the customers to make good decisions depends on the quality of information support they are provided. Our ability to provide quality information depends on the research we do on the basic steps for providing information support.

The steps in information support are (1) identifying and measuring the needs of the customers, (2) collecting and maintaining this information, (3) restructuring and analyzing the data, (4) delivering and reporting the findings, and (5) using the information developed from the data. Systematic research requires considering the issues related to each step of the information support circle shown in Figure 9.1 (McLaughlin and Howard, 1991; McLaughlin and McLaughlin, 1989).

We begin by placing the issues discussed by this volume's authors into each of the five components of the circle. We next develop a list of questions for each component to show the types of information that can be used to evaluate a guidebook. These questions also reveal topics for further research. Inherent to these lists of questions and the structure of the five steps is the potential to develop standards for college guides and rankings, and we propose criteria for these.

Table 9.1 shows the major relationships between some of the primary concerns of the various authors and the five steps of the information support circle. This table shows there are many areas of overlapping concern among the authors. In the following discussion, we expand on these concerns, identify the standard for each step, and list some of the questions that need to be considered to determine if a guide meets the standard.

Figure 9.1. Information Support Circle

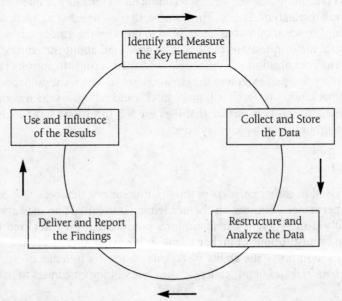

Identify and Measure the Key Elements. Identification and measurement is the process of identifying key elements of the intended use and determining what measures support this use. This component receives substantial attention in this volume from both academicians and publishers. For example, academicians note that we must understand the student choice process model in order to identify what to measure (Hossler and Foley), to identify all important aspects of a college or university (McGuire), to base rankings on chosen criteria (Stuart), to identify adequate measures of quality and cost (Mallette), and to identify measures that represent the broad spectrum of higher education institutions (Mallette). Publishers also discuss the difficulties inherent to data identification and measurement. They acknowledge the difficulty in identifying outcomes measures (Fiske). All agree that students want objective, reliable, credible information when making a choice concerning a college or university.

The relevant criteria for judging identification and measurement of key elements is content validity, or the degree to which a guidebook contains all of the major elements necessary for accomplishing its stated purpose. The following questions should be asked: What is the stated mission or purpose for the guide or ranking? What is the related decision process for the user? How does the publication relate to the components of what is known about this decision process? How are the key components measured or represented or observed? Is there evidence of causal linkage between the measures and the decision process?

In summary, concepts and components related to the purpose of the guide must be identified. The associated measures must be described and verified in order to establish the content validity of the material.

Table 9.1. Summary Analysis of Types of Concerns Expressed by Chapter Authors

Authors	Identify and Measure	Collect and Store	Restructure and Analyze	Deliver and Report	Use and Influence
Hunter		X	X	X	
McGuire	X		X		
Hossler and Foley	X				X
Stuart	X	X		X	
Mallette	X	X	X	X	
Machung		X			X
Hoeritz (P)	X	X			
Corderman (P)		X			
Fiske (P)	X	X			X
Reed (P)					X
Morse (P)	X	X	X	X	
Gilbert (P)	X				X

Note: P = publisher.

Collect and Store the Data. Data must be gathered and maintained in a manner that ensures data reliability. Both academicians and publishers express considerable interest in the problems associated with data collection and maintenance. Academicians argue for systems and processes under which data are not burdensome to collect (Mallette) and for standardized response formats for surveys (Machung). Publishers also call for development of better methods for collecting data. They acknowledge the value of developing standardization for core data (Hoeritz).

On the issue of data definition, Machung notes that "the task of constructing unambiguous definitions that simultaneously fit a large number of different types of institutions, ranging from two-year vocational colleges to large, research-oriented, multicampus multiversities, is daunting." Recognizing this problem, Fiske calls for common agreement on data definitions. Gilbert cautions that one cannot accept institutionally supplied data at face value and suggests a need for verification. The publishers Corderman and Morse argue that they already collect and provide credible data for many publications, and Morse suggests that many colleges lack a consistent internal system for collecting accurate information.

Criteria for judging data collection and storage include collection methods used, the internal consistency of items, stability of scores, and objectivity of reports containing data. After collection, the data need to be handled in a manner that ensures their reliability. The following questions provide a starting point for addressing the collection and storage of the data: Does the procedure described include return rates, sampling method, and follow-up for data that are obtained from surveys? Is rater bias controlled or measured with various criteria? Are institutional and intermediate reports checked for internal consistency and stability? How are missing data handled? What definitions are used and how are they standardized across institutions? Are intermediate summary data available in a manner consistent with security requirements?

In summary, the data must be collected under stable, objective, and standardized conditions. They should be audited to ensure completeness and consistency. Information about the reliability of the data must be available upon request.

Restructure and Analyze the Data. Data restructuring and analysis refers to integrating data from various sources, analyzing the data, summarizing and focusing on issues, and describing the limitations of the data. If these steps are established, then the results can be properly interpreted and the methodology has internal validity.

Both academicians and publishers agree that the guidebook should describe the analytical methods and weighting processes used to compare institutions. By contrast, there is disagreement on the value and usefulness of specific approaches to restructuring and analysis, for example, rankings and rating of institutions. On the one hand, academicians note the problems associated with use of weights and with determining the "best" weighting (McGuire). Mallette cautions that statistical rankings should not be used to imply a degree of precision that masks arbitrary and subjective design decisions. Other academicians suggest doing away with ranking and rating (Hunter). Mallette is highly suspicious of the set of categories, choice of measures, and choice of weights used by publishers. In contrast, publishers argue that people have a right and desire to compare institutions and that rankings are one way of responding to that demand.

The following questions provide a starting point for addressing the restructuring and analysis of the data: How are the data restructured and what are the grounds for various weightings? Are the measures used in ratings and rankings shown to be properly and consistently related to the criterion? What is the stability of the rankings and what has been changed? Do certain groups of institutions have unique practices of reporting data? Were certain institutions excluded from the sample? Do certain sets of variables influence the outcomes for reasons not related to their purpose?

Guidebooks need to fully explain their methodology. The rationale for selecting institutions and weighting measures must be explained and supported.

Deliver and Report the Findings. The issue of delivering the findings to the end user and articulating how that information should be used encompasses concerns for external validity. These concerns, as voiced by academicians in this volume, include the need for a standardized reporting format for information presented to the public (Hunter) and the need for a mechanism for converting data into useful information for public needs (Stuart). Few would disagree with Morse's position that the purpose "is not to publish for a mass readership a document with a long, detailed statistical methodology spelled out." Nevertheless, neither academicians nor publishers seem to support information delivery without description of the methodology. The actual value of the information for specific types of decisions is obviously a topic for continuing debate.

It is also critical to consider the new technologies and their impact on delivery of information. Corderman raises the issue of software, compact disks, and other technology on the home and school desktop. In addition, a multitude of questions are raised in relation to the Internet about the process of delivering data and information on colleges and universities.

The Internet is already becoming filled with various information and data about institutions. Some of the data link to the home pages of the institutions, such as the list of all American universities home pages: <http://www.clas.ufl.edu:80/CLAS/american-universities.html>. Some pages have much more than basic descriptive information. Some help students select majors based on experience, career interest, and skills needed to succeed. Many include the majors provided, and some also provide directories of faculty along with their research interests. Some of the institutions have opportunities for interested parties to provide names and addresses for further information.

In addition, publishers and government agencies use networks. For example, Peterson's and the Princeton Access Guide are two publishers that build home pages. Others are sure to be out there soon. Some state-level agencies are providing data about institutions on state-level home pages and ftp/gopher sites. Basic questions remain concerning how the various types of information can best be delivered to various segments of the market.

The relevant criterion under delivery and report of findings is external validity. The material delivered to the user must support the ability of the user to apply it to specific situations beyond the current point in time and sometimes beyond the current sample of institutions. The following questions provide a starting point: Is the intended use identified and are limitations of the material explained? If groups of institutions are used, are the groups related to the stated use of the guide? Are the results sufficiently timely to support the intended use? Are the results reported in a manner consistent with their reliability and validity? Can the reader find where to obtain clarification or interpretation? Is the delivery consistent with the ability and needs of the intended user?

Use and Influence of the Results. Use and influence refers to how the information is used to clarify a situation, make a decision, or advocate a belief or value. The construct validity of the guide establishes its ability to influence a situation through proper use of relevant information. Throughout this volume, authors emphasize the need to determine how guidebooks influence the college choice decision. Questions concerning the influence of guidebooks on other decisions and on the image of an institution remain largely unanswered.

Academicians raise questions concerning the construct validity of the guides (McGuire). Are the data sufficient and relevant for the intended purpose and use? Other questions surface concerning how much information is actually reaching the intended user (Machung) and the influence it has (Hossler). By contrast, publishers such as Reed note that "the popularity of the directories attests that these guidebooks are the gateway to the application process." This argument is not inconsistent with popular views of how the free-market mechanism works.

However, it is obvious that use of college guidebooks is not yet fully understood. If use is not understood, then a model appropriate for identification of data needed and measurement of those data cannot be constructed. We have come full circle, and there are still numerous, very specific questions to be addressed, questions about unmet needs as well as misdirected conclusions.

The following questions provide a starting point for addressing the use and influence of the results: Is there any evidence that the document has been used in the manner for which it is advertised? Is there any evidence that it has had an influence on decisions of the intended user group? Is the document an end-use product or is it an inducement to obtain additional products? If it is an intermediate product, is the customer so informed at an early stage? What are the costs and benefits to the various suppliers and producers of the data and information? What are the educational, commercial, political, and management uses of the information? If the information is not sufficient and relevant, or is not focused and timely enough to accomplish its stated intent, then it will not have the appropriate use and influence to support its continuance.

Sequential Steps of the Circle. The steps of the circle are sequentially dependent. The quality of each step depends on the quality of the preceding step. For example, until problems associated with identification and measurement and failure to develop a usable model are solved, conflict over rankings or ratings and other problems in the area of data restructuring and analysis will remain. These problems emphasize the need to use a complete framework in the development of a research agenda.

The Larger Picture

"It is tempting to describe the conduct of research as an orderly, sequential process in which we routinely follow a carefully laid out series of steps which ultimately leads to important substantive findings. Yet as any practitioner will readily admit, the research process is not so neat and tidy. Even when following a carefully constructed plan of research, the investigator must inevitably be prepared to adapt his or her research efforts to the unforeseen occurrence, the unanticipated problem, and the serendipitous discovery" (Asher, 1984, p. 3). The information support circle provides a framework to develop research questions for guidebook evaluation. These questions can be used to construct a useful plan of research. However, if contextual process questions about guidebook use are not addressed, progress will be limited and less than permanent. Foremost, we must develop an environment that fosters equitable transactions of effort and value. Research is needed at the process level to remove obstacles that limit positive opportunities for the guides.

In answer to the question "Who are the primary stakeholders in the process of guidebooks and ratings?" we have considered students and parents. We have examined the perspectives of data suppliers. We have considered the perspectives of publishers. We have noted institutional perspectives. Who are the other key stakeholders? Other key groups include legislators, the public, other professions, and those who examine institutional characteristics.

Merely identifying the primary and secondary guidebook stakeholders is not enough, however. We also need to determine the main perspectives of these various stakeholders. These perspectives assign social value. It is simple to ascribe the perspective of scholarly inquiry to the academician, economic self-interest to the publisher, and ethical professionalism to data suppliers. Researchers must anticipate the obviously more complex situation. As some of this volume's authors indicate, our institutions use the guides and ratings for their own economic self-interest, publishers encourage the professional development of those working on guides, and members of our own and other professions respond to scholarly and economic issues as well as to ethical concerns.

Next Steps for Developing Standards for Guidebooks

Once we learn more about the stakeholder environment surrounding college guidebooks, we will be in a better position to continue the development of standards. We say "continue" since, as Hunter notes, the National Association of College Admission Counselors has already started the effort with their *Guide to College Guidebooks,* specifying the roles of the publisher, the institution, and the general public. In addition, authors, such as McGuire, give numerous suggestions for the standards that guidebooks and rankings should meet.

Researchers need to look for the proper structure and infrastructure for such standards. We have proposed a five-step set of standards based on a behavioral science model of reliability and validity. Numerous other alternatives exist. Is it possible to apply some of the concepts of grounded theory and stakeholder analysis? What should be the basis for continued work? It may well be that the standards need to be developed as part of a research process (Strauss and Corbin, 1990).

Who should coordinate the development of the standards? Tradition suggests a consortium of those with a stake in the process and relevant professional skills. Does this exclude those with an economic interest in the standards?

How will the evidence of adherence to standards be developed and presented? Some authors in this volume suggest a loss of credibility by institutional representatives. Other authors question the credibility of some publications ranging from the best seller to the totally obscure. Both publishers and campus officials will need to address the issue of standards, but the evaluation process will need to be determined.

How will standards be enforced? What can be done to encourage various participants to comply with what has been determined as either "essential" or "best practices"? Is it possible to follow the perspective of the American Psychological Association (APA), American Educational Research Association (AERA), and National Council on Measurement in Education (NCME) (1966, p. 9), which concluded that "responsibilities for making inferences as to the meaning and legitimate uses of tests results in a particular setting rests with the user, but in making such judgment he is dependent upon the available information about the tests." This information presumably is provided by the producer. Since almost any test can be used improperly, "primary responsibility for improvement of testing rests on the shoulders of test users. These standards should serve to extend the professional training of these users so that they will make better use of the information about tests and the tests themselves. . . . Publication of superior information about tests by no means guarantees that tests will be used well" (APA, AERA, NCME, 1966, p. 9). If we follow this paradigm, then the standards help the publisher demonstrate the quality of the guide, the user takes responsibility for learning to use the guide, and there is an opportunity for improvement but no guarantee of proper use.

Supporting the development of technical standards requires that institutional researchers work with various stakeholders. This work requires the professional skills of information brokers, a role that we often perform at our institutions. We need to start with research examining specific issues and barriers that limit the ability to develop and implement such standards. This will be a challenge, but it may be the most promising way to reduce the mayhem of the market.

JOSETTA S. MCLAUGHLIN is professor of management at Radford University, Radford, Virginia. Her areas of interest include strategic management and social issues.

GERALD W. MCLAUGHLIN is director of institutional research at Virginia Polytechnic Institute and State University, Blacksburg. His areas of interest include the management of data and methodology of decision making.

REFERENCES

American Psychological Association (APA), American Educational Research Association (AERA), and the National Council on Measurement in Education (NCME). *Standards for Educational and Psychological Tests*. Washington, D.C.: American Psychological Association, 1966.

"America's Best Colleges: 1995 Annual Guide." *U.S. News & World Report*, 1994, *117* (12), 5, 86–119.

Anastasi, A. *Psychological Testing*. (6th ed.) New York: Macmillan, 1988.

Antonoff, S., and Friedemann, M. *College Match: A Blueprint for Choosing the Best School for You*. Alexandria, Va.: Octameron Associates, 1994.

Asher, H. "The Research Process." In H. B. Asher, H. B. Weisberg, J. H. Kessel, and W. P. Shively (eds.), *Theory-Building and Data Analysis in the Social Sciences*. Knoxville: University of Tennessee Press, 1984.

Astin, A. W. *What Matters in College: Four Critical Years Revisited*. San Francisco: Jossey-Bass, 1992.

Astin, A. W., and Solmon, L. C. "Are Reputational Ratings Needed to Measure Quality?" *Change*, 1981, *13* (2), 14–19.

Berman, S. *The Underground Guide to the College of Your Choice*. New York: Signet Books, 1971.

Birnbach, L. *Lisa Birnbach's New and Improved College Book*. Englewood Cliffs, N.J.: Prentice Hall, 1992.

Blau, P. M., and Margulies, R. Z. "The Reputation of American Professional Schools." *Change*, 1974–1975, *6* (10), 42–47.

Bogue, E. G., and Saunders, R. L. *The Evidence for Quality: Strengthening the Tests of Academic and Administrative Effectiveness*. San Francisco: Jossey-Bass, 1992.

Boyer, E. L. *College: The Undergraduate Experience in America*. New York: HarperCollins, 1987.

Boyer, E. L. "Exploring the Future: Seeking New Challenges." *Journal of College Admissions*, 1988, *118*, 2–8.

Carmody, D. "Colleges' SAT Lists Can Be Creative Works." *New York Times*, Nov. 25, 1987, p. E10.

Carnegie Foundation for the Advancement of Teaching. *A Classification of Institutions of Higher Education*. Princeton, N.J.: Carnegie Foundation for the Advancement of Teaching, 1994.

Carter, D. J., and Wilson, R. *Minorities in Higher Education: 1994*. Thirteenth Annual Status Report. Washington, D.C.: American Council on Education, 1995.

Cartter, A. M. *An Assessment of Quality in Graduate Education*. Washington, D.C.: American Council on Education, 1966.

Cass, M., and Cass-Liepmann, J. *Cass & Birnbaum's Guide to American Colleges*. New York: HarperCollins, 1994.

Cattell, J. M. *American Men of Science*. (2nd ed.) New York: Science Press, 1910.

Cattell, J. M. *American Men of Science*. (5th ed.) New York: Science Press, 1933.

Chait, R. P. "The Future of Academic Tenure." *Priorities*, 1995, *3*, 1–11.

Chapman, D. "A Model of Student College Choice." *Journal of Higher Education*, 1981, *52* (5), 490–505.

Clark, C. R., and Hossler, D. "Marketing in Nonprofit Organizations." In D. Hossler, J. P. Bean, and Associates, *The Strategic Management of College Enrollments*. San Francisco: Jossey-Bass, 1990.

Coggeshall, P. E. "Response to the Rankings." *Change*, 1992, *24* (6), 46–53.

College Admissions Data Handbook. New Orleans: Wintergreen/Orchard House, 1994.

College Entrance Examination Board Annual Survey of Colleges, 1994–95. New York: College Entrance Examination Board, 1994.

College Research Group. *The Right College.* New York: Arco, 1992.

Cuseo, J. B. *Assessing College Quality: Perennial Myths, Misleading Media Rankings, Alternative Criteria, and Methodologies.* Rancho Palos Verdes, Calif.: Marymount College, 1994a.

Cuseo, J. B. *The Empirical Case Against College Rankings: Research and Scholarship Refuting the Quality Criteria Used by Mass-Media Magazines.* Rancho Palos Verdes, Calif.: Marymount College, 1994b.

Cuseo, J. B. *Minimizing the Negative Impact of Mass-Media College Rankings: Suggested Strategies for High School, Independent, and College Admission Counselors.* Rancho Palos Verdes, Calif.: Marymount College, 1994c.

Drew, D. E., and Karpf, R. "Ranking Academic Departments: Empirical Findings and a Theoretical Perspective." *Research in Higher Education,* 1981, *14,* 305–320.

"First Tier: College Guides Give Wake Forest Top Grades." *Wake Forest University Magazine,* Dec. 1994, p. 3.

Fleming, J. *Blacks in College: A Comparative Study of Students' Success in Black and White Institutions.* San Francisco: Jossey-Bass, 1984.

Ford, S. "To Hear the Cheers, UNC Campuses Must Excel." *News & Observer,* Oct. 2, 1994, p. 22A.

Friedland, L. "Great Ski Colleges." *Ski,* 1987, *52,* 50–56.

Galotti, K. M., and Kozberg, S. F. "Adolescents' Experience of a Life Framing Decision." *Journal of Youth and Adolescence,* in press.

Galotti, K. M., and Mark, M. C. "How Do High School Students Structure an Important Life Decision? A Short-Term Longitudinal Study of the College Decision-Making Process." *Research in Higher Education,* 1994, *35* (5), 589–607.

Gilbert, J. "Satisfying a Hunger for Information." *College Board Review,* 1992, *163,* 16–36.

Gilley, J. W. "Faust Goes to College." *Academe,* 1992, *78* (3), 9–11.

Gilmore, J. *Price and Quality in Higher Education.* Office of Educational Research and Improvement, U.S. Department of Education. Washington, D.C.: Government Printing Office, 1991.

Gose, B. "Second Thoughts at Women's Colleges." *Chronicle of Higher Education,* Feb. 10, 1995, pp. A22–A24.

Gourman, J. *The Gourman Report: A Rating of Undergraduate Programs in American and International Universities.* Los Angeles: National Education Standards, 1993.

Greene, H., and Minton, R. *Scaling the Ivy Wall: 12 Winning Steps to College Admissions.* Boston: Little, Brown, 1987.

Hamrick, F. A., and Hossler, D. "The Use of Diverse Information Gathering Methods in the Postsecondary Decision-Making Process." *Review of Higher Education,* 1996, *19* (2), 55–74.

Hossler, D. "Choosing Colleges: A Summary of a Four-Year Study of College Choice." Paper presented at the Association of American Collegiate Registrars and Admissions Officers Enrollment Management Conference, Atlanta, Nov. 1991.

Hossler, D., Braxton, J., and Coopersmith, G. "Understanding Student College Choice." In J. C. Smart (ed.), *Higher Education: Handbook of Theory and Research.* Vol. 5. New York: Agathon, 1989.

Hossler, D., and Litten, L. H. *Mapping the Higher Education Landscape.* New York: College Entrance Examination Board, 1993.

Hossler, D., Schmit, J., Vesper, N., and Bouse, G. *A Longitudinal Study of the Postsecondary Plans and Activities of Indiana High School Students and Their Parents.* Final Report to the Lilly Endowment. Bloomington: Indiana University, 1992.

Hossler, D., and Vesper, N. "The Changing Importance of College Attributes: A Longitudinal Study." Paper presented at the annual meeting of the American Educational Research Association, Chicago, Apr. 1991.

Hughes, R. M. *A Study of the Graduate Schools of America.* Oxford, Ohio: Miami University Press, 1925.

Hunter, B. *Hunter's Guide to the College Guides*. Naples, Fla.: Bruce Hunter, 1994.

Huntington, R., and Ochsner, N. "Surveys for College Guidebooks: A Guide to Guide Usage." *Maryland 2000: Journal of the Maryland Association for Institutional Research*, 1993, 2, 55–63.

Johnson, R., and Wichern, D. *Applied Multivariate Statistical Analysis*. (3rd ed.) Englewood Cliffs, N.J.: Prentice Hall, 1992.

Jones, L. V., Lindzey, G., and Coggeshall, P. E. (eds.). *Assessment of Research-Doctorate Programs in the United States*. Washington, D.C.: National Academy of Science Press, 1982.

Kasky, J. "Duke Beats the Top 25 Football Schools, but Check Caltech." *Money*, 1995, 24 (1), 20.

Knowlton, S. "Hyping Numbers at Colleges." *New York Times*, Jan. 8, 1995, pp. A48–A49.

Kotler, P., and Fox, K. *Strategic Marketing for Educational Institutions*. Englewood Cliffs, N.J.: Prentice Hall, 1985.

Krevolin, J. K., and Smerd, S. *Which College Is Best for You? A Workbook for Selecting and Getting into the College of Your Choice*. New York: Arco, 1984.

"Letters to the Editor." *Wall Street Journal*, Apr. 27, 1995, p. A15.

Litten, L. H. "Perspectives on Pricing." In D. Hossler (ed.), *Managing College Enrollments*. New Directions for Higher Education, no. 53. San Francisco: Jossey-Bass, 1986.

Litten, L. H., and Hall, A. E. "In the Eyes of Our Beholders: Some Evidence on How High School Students and Their Parents View Quality in Colleges." *Journal of Higher Education*, 1989, 60, 302–324.

Litten, L. H., Sullivan, D., and Brodigan, D. L. *Applying Market Research to College Admissions*. New York: College Entrance Examination Board, 1983.

McDonough, P. M. "Buying and Selling Higher Education: The Social Construction of the College Applicant." *Journal of Higher Education*, 1994, 65, 427–446.

McDonough, P. M., and Robertson, L. "Gatekeepers or Marketers: Reclaiming the Educational Role of Chief Admission Officers." *Journal of College Admissions*, 1995, 147, 22–31.

McLaughlin, G., and Howard, R. "Check the Quality of Your Information Support." *CAUSE/EFFECT*, 1991, 14 (1), 23–27.

McLaughlin, G., and McLaughlin, J. "Barriers to Information Use: The Organizational Context." In P. T. Ewell (ed.), *Enhancing Information Use in Decision Making*. New Directions for Institutional Research, no. 64. San Francisco: Jossey-Bass, 1989.

Margulies, R. Z., and Blau, P. M. "America's Leading Professional Schools." *Change*, 1973, 5 (9), 21–27.

Meltzer, T., Knower, Z., Custard, E. T., and Katzman, J. *The Princeton Review Student Access Guide to the Best 306 Colleges*. New York: Villard Books, 1994.

Moll, R. *The Public Ivys*. New York: Viking Penguin, 1985.

Moll, R. *Playing the Selective College Admissions Game*. New York: Penguin Books, 1994.

Money Guide: America's Best College Buys. New York: Money Magazine, 1990.

Money Guide: Your Best College Buys Now, 1995. New York: Money Magazine, 1994.

Morrow, D. "A Better Indicator." *Smart Money*, Dec. 1994, pp. 31–33.

National Association of College Admission Counselors (NACAC). *Membership Directory and Association Policies, 1994–95*. Alexandria, Va.: National Association of College Admission Counselors, 1994.

National Center for Education Statistics. *Digest of Education Statistics*. Washington, D.C.: Government Printing Office, 1994.

National Institute of Standards and Technology. *Malcolm Baldrige National Quality Award: Education Pilot Criteria: 1995*. Washington, D.C.: Government Printing Office, 1994.

Nemko, M. "A Blueprint for a Truly Useful College Guide." *Chronicle of Higher Education*, Feb. 3, 1993, pp. B3–B4.

Nicholson, J. M. "A Guide to the College Guides: Or How to Find a College, in 25 Easy Volumes." *Change*, 1983, 15 (1), 16–21, 46–50.

Nicholson, J. M. "A Guide to the Guides." *Change*, 1991, 23 (6), 23–29.

Pascarella, E. T., and Terenzini, P. T. *How College Affects Students: Findings and Insights from Twenty Years of Research*. San Francisco: Jossey-Bass, 1991.

Paulsen, M. B. *College Choice: Understanding Student Enrollment Behavior.* ASHE-ERIC Higher Education Report No. 6. Washington, D.C.: Association for the Study of Higher Education, 1990.

Pollock, C. R. "College Guidebooks—Users Beware." *Journal of College Admissions,* 1992, *135,* 21–28.

Pope, L. *Looking Beyond the Ivy League: Finding the College That's Right for You.* New York: Penguin Books, 1990.

Quigley, S. "On the Lighter Side." *Journal of College Admission,* 1992, *137,* 2.

Reeves, S., and Marriott, A. "A Burst of Popularity." *U.S. News & World Report,* 1994, *117* (12), 105–108.

Rich, S. "Ratings and Rankings: Task Force Meets in Baltimore." *North East Association for Institutional Research Newsletter,* Winter 1995, p. 4.

Roose, K. D., and Anderson, C. J. *A Rating of Graduate Programs.* Washington, D.C.: American Council on Education, 1970.

Rothkopf, A. "Devising Better Ways to Measure the Quality of Colleges and Universities." *Chronicle of Higher Education,* July 14, 1995, p. B3.

Roueche, J. E., and Baker, G. A., III. *Access and Excellence: The Open-Door College.* Washington, D.C.: Community College Press, 1987.

Rubenstone, S., and Dalby, S. *College Admissions: A Crash Course for Panicked Parents.* New York: Macmillan, 1994.

Rugg, F. *Rugg's Recommendations on the Colleges.* Sarasota, Fla.: Rugg's Recommendations, 1994.

Sanoff, A. P. "College Guide Tells Methods for Rankings." *New York Times,* Jan. 14, 1995, p. A18.

Schmit, J. "An Empirical Look at the Search Stage of the Student College Choice Model." Unpublished doctoral dissertation, Department of Educational Leadership and Policy Studies, Indiana University, 1991.

Shepard, L. A. "Evaluating Test Validity." In T. F. Donlon (ed.), *The College Board Technical Handbook for the Scholastic Aptitude Test and Achievement Tests.* New York: College Entrance Examination Board, 1984.

Simon, H. A. *Models of My Life.* New York: Basic Books, 1991.

Solorzano, L. *Barron's Best Buys in College Education.* New York: Barron's Educational Series, 1992.

Stecklow, S. "Colleges Inflate SATs and Graduation Rates in Popular Guidebooks." *Wall Street Journal,* Apr. 5, 1995, pp. A1, A4, A8.

Straughn, C. T., II, and Lovejoy-Straughn, B. *Lovejoy's College Guide.* (22nd ed.) Englewood Cliffs, N.J.: Prentice Hall, 1993.

Strauss, A., and Corbin, J. *Basics of Grounded Theory Methods.* Thousand Oaks, Calif.: Sage, 1990.

Swoboda, F. " 'Glass Ceiling' Firmly in Place, Panel Finds." *Washington Post,* Mar. 16, 1995, pp. A1, A18.

Talbot, M. "Where the Boys Aren't: What's Right—and Wrong—with Women's Colleges Today." *Washington Post Magazine,* Nov. 20, 1994, pp. 12–35.

Tan, D. L. "A Multivariate Approach to the Assessment of Quality." *Research in Higher Education,* 1992, *33* (2), 205–226.

Terenzini, P. T. "Some Myths About Undergraduate Education." *SHEEO/NCES Network News,* 1994, *13* (4), 3–4.

Terenzini, P. T., and Pascarella, E. T. "Living with Myths: Undergraduate Education in America." *Change,* 1994, *26* (1), 28–32.

Theus, K. T. "Academic Reputations: The Process of Formation and Decay." *Public Relations Review,* 1993, *19* (3), 277–291.

"Top 100 Degree Producers." *Black Issues in Higher Education,* 1995, *12* (7), 38–73.

Webster, D. S. "America's Highest Ranked Graduate Schools, 1925–1982." *Change,* 1983, *15* (4), 14–24.

Webster, D. S. "Innovation in Ph.D. Programs and Scores in Reputational Rankings." In M. J. Pelczar, Jr., and L. C. Solman (eds.), *Keeping Graduate Programs Responsive to National Needs.* New Directions for Higher Education, no. 46. San Francisco: Jossey-Bass, 1984a.

Webster, D. S. "Who Is Jack Gourman and Why Is He Saying All Those Things About My College?" *Change,* 1984b, *16* (8), 14–19, 45–56.

Webster, D. S. *Academic Quality Rankings of American Colleges and Universities.* Springfield, Ill.: Thomas, 1986a.

Webster, D. S. "Jack Gourman's Rankings of Colleges and Universities: A Guide for the Perplexed." *Research Quarterly,* 1986b, *25* (3), 323–331.

Webster, D. S. "Academic Rankings: First on a List of One." *Academe,* 1992a, *78* (5), 19–22.

Webster, D. S. "Rankings of Undergraduate Education in *U.S. News & World Report* and *Money:* Are They Any Good?" *Change,* 1992b, *24* (2), 18–31.

Webster, D. S. "Reputational Rankings of Colleges, Universities, and Individual Disciplines and Fields of Study, from Their Beginnings to the Present." In J. C. Smart (ed.), *Higher Education: Handbook of Theory and Research.* Vol. 8. New York: Agathon Press, 1992c.

Webster, D. S., and Conrad, C. F. "Using Faculty Research Performance for Academic Quality Rankings." In J. W. Creswell (ed.), *Measuring Faculty Research Performance.* New Directions for Institutional Research, no. 50. San Francisco: Jossey-Bass, 1986.

Webster, D. S., and Massey, S. W. "The Complete Rankings from the *U.S. News & World Report* 1992 Survey of Doctoral Programs in Six Liberal Arts Disciplines." *Change,* 1992, *24* (6), 20–45.

Wintergreen/Orchard House Survey Form for 1993–94. New Orleans: Wintergreen/Orchard House, 1993.

Wright, B. A. "The Ratings Game: How the Media Affect College Admission." *College Board Review,* 1990–1991, *158,* 12–17, 31–32.

Wright, B. A. "A Little Learning Is a Dangerous Thing: A Look at Two Popular College Rankings." *College Board Review,* 1992, *163,* 6–16.

Yale Daily News. The Insider's Guide to Colleges. New York: St. Martin's Press, 1993.

INDEX

ORDERING INFORMATION

NEW DIRECTIONS FOR INSTITUTIONAL RESEARCH is a series of paperback books that provides planners and administrators in all types of academic institutions with guidelines in such areas as resource coordination, information analysis, program evaluation, and institutional management. Books in the series are published quarterly in spring, summer, fall, and winter and are available for purchase by subscription as well as by single copy.

SUBSCRIPTIONS for 1995 cost $48.00 for individuals (a savings of 29 percent over single-copy prices) and $64.00 for institutions, agencies, and libraries. Please do not send institutional checks for personal subscriptions. Standing orders are accepted.

SINGLE COPIES cost $19.00 plus shipping (see below) when payment accompanies order. California, New Jersey, New York, and Washington, D.C., residents please include appropriate sales tax. Canadian residents add GST and any local taxes. Billed orders will be charged shipping and handling. No billed shipments to post office boxes. Orders from outside the United States or Canada *must be prepaid* in U.S. dollars or charged to VISA, MasterCard, or American Express.

SHIPPING (SINGLE COPIES ONLY): one issue, add $3.50; two issues, add $4.50; three issues, add $5.50; four to five issues, add $6.50; six to seven issues, add $7.50; eight or more issues, add $8.50.

DISCOUNTS FOR QUANTITY ORDERS are available. Please write to the address below for information.

ALL ORDERS must include either the name of an individual or an official purchase order number. Please submit your order as follows:
   Subscriptions: specify series and year subscription is to begin
   Single copies: include individual title code (such as IR78)

MAIL ALL ORDERS TO:
   Jossey-Bass Publishers
   350 Sansome Street
   San Francisco, CA 94104-1342

FOR SUBSCRIPTION SALES OUTSIDE OF THE UNITED STATES, CONTACT: any international subscription agency or Jossey-Bass directly.

OTHER TITLES AVAILABLE IN THE
NEW DIRECTIONS FOR INSTITUTIONAL RESEARCH SERIES
Patrick T. Terenzini, Editor-in-Chief